The Way, the Truth and the Life Series

Teacher's Book 1

Authors: Sr. Marcellina Cooney CP and Amette Ley

Editorial Team: Maire Buonocore, Angela Edwards, Hattie Elwes, Susan Lawless, Tracy McGovern Hill, Kerry Malone, Linda O'Brien, Kathleen Richards

Teachers' Enterprise in Religious Education Co. Ltd

Teacher Book 1

Published by: Teachers' Enterprise in Religious Education Co. Ltd

Nihil obstat: Father Anton Cowan – Censor.

Imprimatur: The Most Rev. Vincent Nichols, Archbishop of Westminster, 22 February 2011, Feast of the Chair of St. Peter.

The Nihil obstat *and* Imprimatur *are a declaration that the books and contents of the Student's Book are free from doctrinal or moral error. It is not implied that those who have granted the* Nihil obstat *and the* Imprimatur *agree with the contents, opinions or statements expressed.*

Design, compilation and format: Ian Curtis, First Sight Graphics, www.firstsightgraphics.com

Printed by: The Magazine Printing Company plc - www.magprint.co.uk

Design and Text copyright © Marcellina Cooney CP.

Theological Adviser: Fr. Herbert Alphonso SJ

Permission credits: Mille Image d'Évangile by Jean-François Kieffer

Front cover: The Annunciation © Jenny Williams

Illustrations: © Jenny Williams; © Norman Young; © Debbie Clark, Beehive Illustration. Photos page 5 & 9 © Lorenzo Lees; page 18 © Sr. Marcellina Cooney CP

All Rights reserved. Apart from the worksheets, no part of this publication may be reproduced or transmitted in any form or by any means without permission in writing from the publisher.

INTRODUCTION

Welcome to the second edition of *'The Way, the Truth & the Life'* Book 1.

The great strength of this series is its simplicity and clarity. It is attractive, lively and appealing to both teachers and pupils.

The Syllabus is based on the Religious Education Curriculum Directory and, therefore, the contents of the Teacher's Book, Big Book and Pupil's Work Book fulfil the requirements of the Bishops' Conference for Religious Education in Catholic schools.

The Teacher's Book provides theological notes, stories, a large variety of activities, guidance on assessment and suggestions for questions on the Big Book. There is also a variety of supporting resources such as websites and songs. The very attractive Pupil's Work Book should encourage children to take pride in their work and be able to share it with their families.

This project is the fruit of wonderful collaboration and hard work of a number of teachers across the country. I thank them for the contribution they are making to curriculum development in Religious Education. I would also like to warmly thank Fr. Herbert Alphonso SJ for his involvement as theological adviser and for the encouragement and support he has given to all involved.

I am confident that all who use this Teacher's Book 1, the corresponding Big Book and Pupil's Work Book will find them a direct, clear help in the important task of enabling their pupils to learn about the Catholic faith and to respond to its invitation with growing faith and love.

✠ Vincent Nichols
Archbishop of Westminster

Teacher Book 1

NOTES FOR USERS

This **Teacher's Book** is accompanied by a **Big Book** and a **Pupil's Work Book** and is based on the **Key Stage 1 Syllabus.** These resources cover all the essential content of the Religious Education Curriculum Directory of the Bishops' Conference of England and Wales at an appropriate level for 5-6 year olds.

The **Syllabus** incorporates two attainment targets: learning *about* the Catholic faith (AT1) and learning *from* Catholic faith (AT2). These are set out in the form of specific key learning objectives for each module and listed in the Teacher's Book.

There are **Scripture texts and notes for Teachers** at the beginning of each section based on the key learning objective. These are intended to enrich the teachers' understanding of the content they are about to teach.

The **'Key Questions'** should be shared with the children at some point so that by the end of the session they will be able to answer them; this provides an assessment exercise.

It is not intended that a key learning objective is covered in each lesson with all the accompanying activities. This may take several lessons and the teacher is free to select the most appropriate tasks for the class. Throughout the year, it is essential to make links between the content covered in religious education and other areas of learning as well as what is happening in the classroom and playground.

When a lighted candle is used teachers should take the necessary precautions, such as, having a fire blanket at hand. For all practical activities, teachers should follow the school's policy and guidance with regard to health and safety and are advised to check the suitability of websites listed in this book before recommending them to children.

CONTENTS

Introduction..................3

Notes for Users..............4

Overview of Syllabus.........6

Methodology..................7

1. God's Great Plan..........8
Key Learning Objectives
Theological Notes
Scripture text and notes for Teachers
Key Questions
Links with Big Book
Text to read to children with questions
Activities

2. Mary our Mother........26
Key Learning Objectives
Theological Notes
Scripture text and notes for Teachers
Key Questions
Links with Big Book
Text to read to children with questions
Activities
Worksheets

3. Families & Celebrations........50
Key Learning Objectives
Theological Notes
Scripture text and notes for Teachers
Key Questions
Links with Big Book
Text to read to children with questions
Activities

4. Following Jesus..........70
Key Learning Objectives
Theological Notes
Scripture text and notes for Teachers
Key Questions
Links with Big Book
Text to read to children with questions
Activities
Worksheet

5. The Resurrection........90
Key Learning Objectives
Theological Notes
Scripture text and notes for Teachers
Key Questions
Links with Big Book
Text to read to children with questions
Activities
Worksheets

6. Miracles..................112
Key Learning Objectives
Theological Notes
Scripture text and notes for Teachers
Key Questions
Links with Big Book
Text to read to children with questions
Activities

Assessment for Learning..............129

Guide to Levels of Achievement...130

Glossary for Pupils......................132

Overview of Foundation and Key Stage One Syllabus

	Autumn 1	Autumn 2	Spring 1	Spring 2	Summer 1	Summer 2
Foundation	F1 God's World	F2 God's Family	F3 Getting to know Jesus	F4 Sorrow & Joy	F5 New Life	F6 Church
Year 1	1.1 God's Great Plan	1.2 Mary our Mother	1.3 Families & Celebrations	1.4 Following Jesus	1.5 The Resurrection	1.6 Miracles
Year 2	2.1 Chosen People	2.2 Mysteries	2.3 The Good News	2.4 The Mass	2.5 Eastertide	2.6 Birth of the Church

METHODOLOGY

Our main focus in this book is to help children to begin to understand the religious content specified by the Religious Education Curriculum Directory [RECD] for this age group. Our aim is also to help children grow in awareness that God comes to us every day in persons, events and situations, and lovingly challenges us to open our hearts to receive Him and allow Him to help us.

Children will need constant help to relate what they are learning to their own lives. There will be opportunities to show them what it means to be part of a family where each person is accepted and loved the way that person is with all his/her limitations and weaknesses. Incidents in the daily life of the classroom and playground will provide opportunities for children to experience the love and care of adults. They will then be able to help children to understand that God is our Father in heaven and to think about what this means for us.

It is essential to start with the children's experience, explore it and build on it and then connect it to the religious content. An example of this would be, when explaining that God made the world, the children and teacher could bring in something that they have made to put on display. The children should be encouraged to talk about how and why we make things and how we feel about them. The next step is to draw attention to all the things God has made: flowers, trees, sky, birds, sky, sun and so on. This leads to a sharing of the story of creation in Genesis through drama, role-play, music, Power Point presentations, art etc.

When teaching miracles to Year 1, great care needs to be taken to explain that miracles are not magic. Miracles are signs, signs of God's power, worked because of God's compassionate and healing love; these signs call for and demand 'faith'. They are seen as signs pointing to who Jesus is. Jesus has this power because he is God the Son. He showed his power because he wanted people to believe and trust in him.

With very young children it is important to concentrate on the motive for miracles (usually compassionate love) rather than *over-emphasising* the supernatural element.

Miracles are not magic. Magic is about control, about illusion, a trick. A miracle is never worked just for our curiosity or entertainment (like 'magic tricks') but to arouse and deepen faith in God and Jesus.

For this age group, it is *not* appropriate to go into details of the crucifixion of Jesus. It is best just to mention it and to put the emphasis on the resurrection. The aim is to help children grasp that Jesus' death and resurrection are together one single mystery of Jesus handing himself over in love to God and to us. One day we will die but we believe that we too will rise from the dead and be in heaven with Jesus.

God's Great Plan

1.1 God's Great Plan

Religious Education Curriculum Directory
"Creation is the first and universal revelation of God's love. As the action of Father, Son and Holy Spirit, creation is the first step towards the covenant relationship God seeks with every human being" (p. 14).

AT1 & AT2
Learning ABOUT and learning FROM the Catholic Faith

Key Learning Objectives
In this unit you will have the opportunity to:

- Be aware of the beauty of God's world.
  - Explore and respond to the wonders of creation e.g. the seasons.

- Hear about the story of Creation from Genesis.
  - Talk about its meaning.

- Know that God made us because He loves us but the first people, Adam and Eve, made some wrong choices.
  - Think of how we can show our love for God.

- Be aware that we have a responsibility to look after God's world.
  - Think of ways we can care for the world.

- Hear an appropriate part of the story of Noah and the Flood.
  - Think about its promise and hope.

THEOLOGICAL NOTES

Q. What does the Church teach about Creation?
Christian tradition from the earliest times has attributed to God the Father the work of creation – the creation of the whole universe. As we profess in the Apostles' Creed: "I believe in God the Father Almighty, Creator of heaven and earth", or in the Nicene Creed: We believe in one God, the Father, the Almighty, maker of heaven and earth, of all that is seen and unseen". So **God the Father** is acknowledged as **the Creator and Origin of all things**, seen and unseen, in the entire cosmos.

One immediate consequence of this fundamental Christian belief for the whole range of our practical Christian living is that we should **give God a real and serious chance to be God** in our lives. And this, not just globally as it were in one all-encompassing act performed once and for all, but in the several daily details of our everyday living. As the celebrated mystic of the 14th century, Meister Eckhart, admirably couched this practical challenge: 'Let go, let God'.

God's Great Plan

Q. Why are there two accounts of Creation?
There are two traditions behind the chapters 1-11, the Priestly (P) and the Yahwist (j).

In Genesis 1, the Priestly creation account is a mature statement of faith about God's relationship with the world and with the creatures in it. This story shows that God's purpose is written into creation – a purpose of order, beauty and obedience as opposed to chaos.

In Genesis 2, the Yahwist creation story is a dramatic account of creation and fall. The characters are representative. Both accounts of creation use the language and imagery of the ancient Mesopotamian myths, but the accounts are adapted to convey the faith of Israel and refute the message of the pagan myths.

Q. What was the first sin?
"When tempted by the devil, the first man and woman allowed trust in their Creator to die in their hearts. In their disobedience they wished to become 'like God' but without God and not in accordance with God (Gen: 3:5). Thus Adam and Eve immediately lost for themselves and for all their descendants the original grace of holiness and justice." (Compendium Catechism of the Catholic Church 75)

Q. What is Original Sin?
The first sin known as "original sin, in which all human beings are born, is the state of deprivation of original holiness and justice …. it remains a mystery which we cannot fully understand." (Compendium Catechism of the Catholic Church 76)

Q. How does the account of Original Sin help us?
It tells us that our human nature has been 'wounded' by original sin. While original sin is removed when we receive the Sacrament of Baptism, we still we suffer from the effects of that sin, that is, we are left with a tendency towards sin.

Here are some examples.
We experience feelings of envy, the desire to dominate others or to 'get even' when things go wrong.

We have a tendency to be selfish, that is, just to think of what we want for ourselves and not to consider the needs of others.

In a subtle way, we can convince ourselves that we have acted justly when we have not faced the truth!

We recognise great injustice in the world but have difficulty remedying it.
We know now that these evil tendencies are not from God; they are the result of the first act of disobedience and selfishness by our first parents. Fortunately, the Bible goes on to explain how God works in wonderful ways to restore our friendship with Him.

Q. What is the importance of Noah and the Flood
The account of Noah and the Flood is the promise of God's unchangeable and faithful love. It reinforces the concept of God's love and care for us and for all creation, and links the physical world - in this case the rainbow - to its meaning.

God's Great Plan

God's Great Plan

> Be aware of the beauty of God's world.
> Explore and respond to the wonders of creation, e.g. the seasons.

Notes for Teachers

God creates and sustains
The scriptures and the teaching of the Church tell us that:
- God is responsible for everything in creation;
- God created out of nothing;
- nothing exists that does not owe its existence to God the Creator;
- because God is infinitely good, creation reflects His goodness;
- God created humankind in His own image and likeness;
- God made humankind the stewards of creation.

We believe that everything that exists is totally dependent upon God's power. That power of creation is expressed in the Book of Genesis in the words: **'Let there be light'**, and there was light. In the same way, if God were to say: 'Let something stop being ...' it would cease to be. In other words, the whole of creation and each one of us depend wholly on God creating and looking after us.

The creation story in Genesis
The people of the Old Testament wanted to know about the creation of the universe. In order to help their readers to understand the mysterious action of God, the writers of Genesis used symbolic stories to get across important **theological truths**.

KEY QUESTIONS (To share with children at any point)
Why do you think God made the world?
Why do you think God made so many beautiful things?

Introductory Activity
Children (and teacher) bring in something they have made to put on the display table. Talk about how and why we make things; how we feel about them and why we want to make them beautiful.

Behind this table prepare to make a wall display that will be built up in the coming weeks. Put **key questions** on display board and put blank bubbles for children's responses which can be filled in when ready.

Link Sentence
Today, we are going to hear a story from the Bible about why God made the world.

God's Great Plan

Look at the picture on page 3 of the Big Book: God's Great Plan

> God's world is very beautiful.
>
> He has made the world for us to live in.
>
> We say 'thank you' to God for His wonderful world.

Questions to ask about Big Book Picture

- What can you see in the picture? *[Encourage children to notice small details, flowers, birds, insects, as well as large features].*

- Have you ever seen [mountains, the sea, etc] yourself? *[Encourage stories of what the children have experienced].*

- Which part of the picture do you think is the most beautiful? Why? *[Encourage children to explore their reasons for considering something beautiful, for instance the colour, the size, how it makes them feel, if it reminds them of something.]*

- Why do you think God made the world such a beautiful place?

- Close your eyes for just a moment. *[When children are quiet]*
  Can you think inside your head of the most beautiful thing you have ever seen?

Perhaps the most beautiful thing you have ever seen was:
- a sunset,
- a tiny baby,
- the waves crashing onto the beach,
- a small cuddly kitten,
- your mum's face when she smiles,
- the stars at night? *[Teacher could add some more here or make a Power Point presentation with images from the Web.]*

Have you ever said 'thank you' to God for all the beautiful things he has made in the world? Let's just take a moment now to say 'thank you' to God in our hearts.
[A moment's silence, depending on mood of class]

God's Great Plan

Activities

1. Invite children to listen to Beethoven's Pastoral Symphony 6 played very softly while Psalm 104 is read. They could interpret this psalm through dance.

   Psalm 104 [adapted]
   God our Father
   You made the great mountains and the sea,
   You made the rivers and the fields and the trees,
   You made the animals and the birds and the fish,
   You made the sun and the moon and the stars,
   You made the rain and the wind,
   You made the frost and the snow,
   We thank you for your wonderful world.

2. Children choose their favourite beautiful things, one large and one small beautiful thing, from the picture in the Big Book or elsewhere and draw them. More able children may be able to construct short sentences to say why they have chosen this. Part of the sentence could be printed: "I chose the …. because….."

3. **CIRCLE TIME** with a big '**THANK YOU**' card and **Candle**
   Let's take time to thank God for the beautiful things he has made.
   God our Father
   We thank you for this wonderful world.
   You made it for us to live in.
   We are very happy to be here.
   Help us to take care of all the beautiful things you have made. Amen

4. With the help of a visualiser, use pictures on pages 3 and 4 of the Big Book to ask questions, e.g. 'I wonder why God made the world?'; 'I wonder why God made so many beautiful things?'

5. **Extension task:** From a selection of pictures [from magazines, posters, even scenes from travel videos] help children to identify 'amazing' features of the world that they were unfamiliar with. Make a 'Did you know?' display, e.g. Did you know that some mountains are so high up that there is always snow on the top of them? Include local features.

6. Show Power Point presentation of the 'Seasons'. Available from the Teachers' Enterprise in Religious Education, 40 Duncan Terrace, London N1 8AL; email: info@tere.org; tel. 020 7359 2642.

God's Great Plan

Story of Creation

> Hear about the story of Creation from Genesis.
> Reflect on its meaning.

Scripture text for Teachers

The first account of the creation
"In the beginning, God created the heavens and the earth. Now the earth was a formless void, there was darkness over the deep, and God's spirit hovered over the water.

God said, 'Let there be light', and there was light. God said that light was good, and God divided light from darkness. God called light 'day', and darkness he called 'night'. Evening came and morning came: the first day.

God said, 'Let there be a vault in the waters to divide the waters in two'. And so it was. God made the vault, and it divided the waters above the vault from the waters under the vault. God called the vault 'heaven'. Evening came and morning came: the second day.

God said, 'Let the waters under heaven come together into a single mass, and let dry land appear'. And so it was. God called the dry land 'earth' and the mass of waters 'seas', and God said that it was good.

God said, 'Let the earth produce vegetation: seed-bearing plants, and fruit trees bearing fruit with their seed inside, on the earth'. And so it was. The earth produced vegetation: plants bearing seed in their several kinds, and trees bearing fruit with their seed inside in their several kinds. God saw that it was good. Evening came and morning came: the third day. (Gen. 1:1-13)

See Gen. 1:14-31 and **2:1-4** for days 4-7.

Key Questions (To share with the children at any point)
Why do you think this is an important story to know?
Why do you think our world keeps going?

Introductory Activity
Have a blue circular cloth on the floor or a table and let the children choose the things they want to put into **their** world. Use pieces of different colour cloth for different parts, e.g. brown for land, green for grass, another shade of blue for sea and use 'small world objects' as well.

Link Sentence
Today, we are going to look at the different things God put into **His** world.

God's Great Plan

Look at the picture on page 4 in Big Book: God Made the World

God made the light, darkness, water and land.

God made trees, plants and animals.

God made people to enjoy them and to look after them.

Question to ask about Big Book picture
What can you see in the picture?

Text to read to children (use objects in a story bag as illustrations).

In the beginning, God made the world and everything in it. He made the sky and the sun and the stars and the moon and all the planets. He made the whole universe out of nothing at all! But to start with, the world was not a place where people could live. God began to make the world ready for us.

First day, God made light and darkness. *[Use black cloth as visual aid for night and silver cloth for day].*

Second day, he made the water and the land separate from each other. *[Use blue cloth for sea and green & brown for land].*

Third day, God made the plants and trees begin to grow. *[add model trees and plants].*

Fourth day, He made the sun and the moon settle into place and there were seasons, summer and autumn, winter and spring. *[Sprinkle moon and star shapes on the cloth].*

Fifth day, God made creatures to live in the sea, and creatures with wings to fly in the air; next He made animals which came to live on the land: noisy monkeys, lumbering elephants, terrible tigers, wriggly snakes, beautiful butterflies etc. God saw it was good and He was very pleased. *[Plastic animals could be added to brown or blue cloth depending on type of animal].*

God's Great Plan

Sixth day, God made something very special. He made people; people to look after the world and all the things in it. *[Use play people]*

Seventh day, now everything was finished and God rested.

Questions to ask:
Why do you think this story is at the beginning of the Bible?

What do you think this story is all about?

I wonder how the world keeps going! *[Leave this as a thought to wonder about. Let the children respond as they wish.]*

Activities
1. Draw a picture for each day to show the different beautiful things God put into His world. See Work Book page 3 'God's Beautiful World'.

2. Work in groups to create a collage of the six days of creation. Each group takes a different day. Use for:
   sequencing;
   discussion;
   display;
   collective act of worship.

3. **Reflective** activity:
   Sit in a circle around a small table.
   Use items from the 'story bag' for children to create a 'Creation Table'.
   Two children slowly walk to the table and put the blue cloth on it while the rest say: 'God made the world'.
   Another child places the silver cloth on the table and children say 'God made light'.
   This is repeated for all the items in the story bag.
   After saying on the last day God rested, the children close their eyes and spend a few moments thinking about the beautiful world God made.

4. Learn **Song**: 'The Wonders I see' by Bernadette Farrell, CD 'Share the Light' Available from Viewpoint Resources Direct, Tel. 020 8692 1138 www.viewpoint24.com

5. ICT for children: www.dottieandbuzz.co.uk click on Creation – you will find a variety of activities.

ICT: http://kids4truth.com/dyna/creation/english.aspx

www.reonline.co.uk click on 'Bible', then 'Creation'.

God's Great Plan

The First People

> Know that God made us because He loves us but the first people, Adam and Eve, made some wrong choices.
> Reflect on God's love for us.

Notes for Teachers
The second account of creation: Gen. 2:5-25
The Fall Gen. 3:1-19

For Year 1 children, it is sufficient to say that Adam and Eve, the first people, made some wrong choices.

Key theological truths in Genesis
- God created man and woman out of love.
- He created them in a state of holiness, which means, in a relationship of friendship with Him.
- God created them in His own image and likeness.
- He gave them the gift of 'freedom', so that they could **freely** be His friends.
- From the very beginning man and woman were given the **freedom** to choose between good and evil.
- God told them to increase and multiply so they became the 'first parents' of all human beings.
- However, our 'first parents' Adam and Eve were tempted by the Evil One.
- They misused their God-given gift of **'freedom'** to turn against their Creator.
- They chose to find their own self-fulfilment apart from God.
- By turning against God they lost their friendship and happiness with Him.
- God had intended His original plan of friendship with Him for all human beings so, because of the disobedience of Adam and Eve, this sin has been passed on to all of us.

KEY QUESTIONS
Why do you think God made us?
How can we show our love for God and take care of each other?

Introductory Activity
Use the items from the 'Home Corner' to role-play people caring for us.
What happens if we don't help each other?

Link Sentence
Today, we are going to hear about the first people who made some wrong choices.

God's Great Plan

Look at the picture on page 4 in the Pupil's Work Book: Adam and Eve

God wants us to be very happy.

But the first people made some wrong choices.

Question to ask about the picture?
Who can you see in the picture?
Why do you think they are looking sad?

Text to read to the Children

When God made the world, it was a very beautiful place. God made the world exactly right for people to live in. When everything was just right, God made the first people. He made a man called Adam and a woman called Eve. God made them because He wanted them to know and love Him. He wanted them to love each other as well. To begin with, Adam and Eve were very happy. They loved God and they loved the world He had made for them.

They took care of each other and they took care of the beautiful world. They gave names to all the animals and they looked after them. They planted seeds in the ground and looked after them and waited until they grew into plants for food. But most important of all, they did what God said and showed their love by looking after each other.

But the time came when they started to make wrong choices. They didn't do what God told them to do. God knew what was best for them, but they didn't listen to Him.

It was a very long time ago that God made those first people. God still loves all the people who live in this beautiful world He has given us. He still wants us all to love Him, to look after each other and to take care of the world around us. Sometimes it is difficult for us to do this. Sometimes we forget to listen to what God has told us and to live the way He would like us to live.

God's Great Plan

Questions to ask on the story
- What are the beautiful things God made for us?

- Why do you think God made us?

- What are the names of the first people God made?

- What were the first things they did? *(They took care of each other and of the beautiful world, etc.)*

- What wrong choice did they make? *(They did not do what God asked them to do.)*

- Sometimes, we make wrong choices. What do you think they might be?

Activities

1. Draw some people who show their love by doing things for you. Write or draw what they do for you.

2. **Work Book** page 4 'Adam and Eve'.

3. Draw two large bubbles. Put the right choices we make in one (with a happy face). Put the wrong choices we make in the other (with a sad face).

4. Display the Key Questions on thought bubbles and spend time with the children reflecting on their responses and then sing a song, e.g.:
   'Love is something if you give it away' Alleluia Book published by A.C. Black

God's Great Plan

God's World

> Be aware that we have a responsibility to look after God's world.
> Think of what we can do not to spoil the world.

Scripture text and notes for Teachers

When God created people, He said:
"Let [them] have dominion over the fish in the sea and over the birds of the air, and over the cattle, and over all the wild animals of the earth, and over every creeping thing that creeps upon the earth". (Gen. 1:26)

We have received the special gift and challenge of sharing in God's creative activity. As 'co-creators', then, our acts should reflect God's own love for creation. So our care for creation can be a true expression of our praise and thanksgiving to God.

Choices of all kinds, environmental, social and personal taken by others long ago affect us now because we all belong to the human family. Choices we make now will affect others in the future.

KEY QUESTIONS [To share with children at any point]
Why do you think God's world got spoilt?
Who do you think should look after God's world?

Introductory Activity
Bring in items for children to choose from e.g. different food
for snack time – apple or banana or choice of toys to play with.

Then move to choices in behaviour which can be role-played.
For example,
Hang coat up or drop it on the floor;
Play with new girl or leave her on her own;
Push along the dinner line or wait your turn.

Discuss with children the results of the different types of behaviour.

Link Sentences
We have been looking at choices. Some choices are not so important, e.g. which toy we play with. But some choices are very important because the way we choose to behave affects God's world and other people.

God's Great Plan

Look at the picture on page 5 in the Big Book: God's World

God has made us a beautiful world to live in.

We all need to help look after it. Sometimes, we forget or don't care.

Then we find the world is not so good to live in.

Questions to ask on picture in Big Book
- What can you see in the picture that is good?
- What is not so good?
- Who has made the 'not so good' things happen?
- Why do you think they did that?
- What could happen to make some of the bad things in the picture a bit better?
- Who could make this happen?
- Is there anything we can do?

Text to read to the Children

Joe and his friends were very excited. They had all been waiting for such a long time for this day to arrive and now, at last, it was here - the day the new school play area would open. Mrs. Ortiz, their teacher, had promised they could all take a turn to use the new equipment. They wouldn't even have to wait until play time. The children all ran into school at top speed – they couldn't wait!

Mrs Ortiz was standing by the classroom door – Joe noticed that she looked rather sad. When everyone had changed their shoes, hung up their coats, were sitting down and the register had been taken, Mrs Ortiz stood up, her face very serious.

"I know how much you were all looking forward to playing in the new area," she said, "but I'm afraid I have bad news. During the night, some people got into the school grounds and damaged the new equipment so badly that it can't be used."

All the children were very quiet. No-one could understand why anyone would want to damage their new play area. They had all worked so hard to raise the money for it – some of their parents had even helped to build it.

God's Great Plan

"What can we do?" asked one of Joe's friends. No-one answered him for a long time. Then Mrs. Allen, the classroom assistant put up her hand.

"We could say a prayer for the people who spoiled our play area," she suggested. "Perhaps they didn't know they should respect the world and the things in it. Perhaps they didn't know that the world and everything in it belongs to God. Then we could begin all over again."

Everyone thought hard about this. Then Mrs Ortiz made the sign of the cross, and all the children joined in with the prayer:

God our Father
Today, some things are not right with our world.
Please help us to forgive those who treated the world, and us, so badly.
Please help us to show them how to look after the world and each other.
Please help us all to begin again with hope for the future.
Amen.

Activities

1. Invite the children to build something from their construction equipment and use two puppets to act as vandals who ruined the playground to destroy their construction.
   - Discuss with the children what the puppets could be saying to each other; what they think and what they feel about it.
   - You could also address questions to the puppets about their behaviour and ask for a reason for it.
   - Children could suggest better choices of behaviour to the puppets to help care for the world.

2. **Work Book** page 5: Looking after God's world. Invite children to make a poster showing how they can look after God's world, e.g. water flowers, look after an animal, feed the birds, pick up litter etc.

3. **Reflection:** Use a globe as a focus for reflection. Children could work individually or in pairs to write a prayer for the world on card. The prayers could then be put around the globe on the floor. Teacher could give children starter sentences, e.g.
   Dear God, help us to ....
   Thank you God for ....

God's Great Plan

Noah's Ark

> Hear an appropriate part of the story of Noah and the Flood.
> Reflect on its promise and hope.

Notes and Scripture text for Teachers

Most of the story of Noah and the Flood is not suitable for young children. A deliberate choice has been made just to tell part of the story with particular reference to the promise. For the whole story see Genesis Chapters 6-9.

The corruption of mankind (Gen. 6:5-12)
Preparation for the flood (Gen. 6:13-22 7:1-16)
The flood (Gen. 7:17-24)
The flood subsides (Gen. 8:1-14)
God tells Noah to disembark (Gen. 8:15-22)
The new world order (9:1-17)
Noah and his sons (9:18-29)

Preparation for the flood
God instructed Noah to build the ark (6:13-22). Then "God said to Noah, 'Go aboard the ark, you and all your household, for you alone among this generation do I see as a good man in my judgement. Of all clean animals you must take seven of each kind, both male and female, of the unclean animals you must take two, a male and its female and of birds of heaven also, seven of each kind, both male and female, to propagate their kind over the whole earth. For in seven days time, I mean to make it rain on the earth for forty days and nights, and I will rid the earth of every living thing that I made'. Noah did all that Yahweh ordered." (7:1-4)

The flood
"The flood lasted forty days on the earth. The waters swelled, lifting the ark until it was raised above the earth. The waters rose and swelled greatly on the earth, and the ark. The waters rose more and more on the earth so that all the highest mountains under the whole of heaven were submerged." (7:17-19)

Eventually when the flood subsided, God made a covenant with Noah and his descendants that there would be no flood to destroy the earth again (9:11). The rainbow is the sign of God's covenant (9:16).

KEY QUESTIONS (To share with children at any point)

Have you ever seen a rainbow?
Do you know the story of the rainbow?
Why do you think God chose a rainbow to remind us of His promise?
What is the promise?

God's Great Plan

Introductory Activity
Teacher to make a promise and keep it, for example, I promise I will come out on duty and give you five minutes extra play tomorrow. I will put this teddy bear on my desk to remind me. When you see the teddy bear you will know I have not forgotten my promise.

Link Sentence
Today, we are going to have a story which is all about a promise that God made and the reminder He gave to us.

Look at the picture on page 6 in the Big Book: Noah's Ark

Noah and his family were God's friends.

God kept them safe from the flood.

God chose the rainbow as a sign of His promise.

Question to ask on Big Book Picture
What can you see in this picture?

Text to read to the Children
Tell this story using the 'Story Box' technique. Cover a shoe box in rainbow colour paper. Inside the box place blue cloth, a toy boat, pairs of animals, dove, small leaf and a rainbow ribbon. Put the lid on the box and ask the children to guess what might be in it. Discuss the colour of the box and its significance. Bring out the items one by one and see if the children can suggest what part they might play in the story. Tell the children you are going to tell them a story and they have to listen for the part each item plays.

One day God spoke to Noah.

"There is going to be a great flood," He said. "You must work hard and build a great ark. You must make it big enough for you and your wife and family and lots of animals and all the food they will need."

So Noah set to work and built the ark. He followed all the instructions God gave him. Just as he finished, it began to rain. It rained harder and harder and harder. Noah and his family and all the animals crowded into the ark with their food.

God's Great Plan

It rained even harder, and soon the ark began to float on the flood water. It rained for forty days. It was an enormous flood – Noah and his family couldn't see any dry land at all.

At last the rain stopped, but it took a lot longer for the flood water to begin to dry up. Noah hoped there would soon be some dry land for the ark to stop on so they could all get out again. He went down inside the ark and found one of the doves they had taken with them. He carried it carefully outside and let it go. Noah and his family waited as the dove flew out over the water and on out of sight. They waited all day until evening came. Then, at last, the dove came flying back to the ark. And in her beak was something wonderful – a fresh olive leaf!

Noah and his family were delighted. A fresh leaf meant there was a tree growing somewhere – on dry land. Life was beginning again.

After a while Noah could see the land and the ark stopped floating and rested on it. Noah and his family and all the animals climbed out.

God spoke to Noah again.

"When it rains again, look up at the beautiful rainbow. When you see the rainbow, remember that I love you and I will never again let the flood waters destroy the whole world."

And even today, when we see a rainbow in the sky, we remember God's promise of love and care to Noah and to all his people.

Questions to ask on the story:

- How do you think Noah felt when God told him there was going to be a flood? *[Fear, worry, trust....]*

- Why do you think Noah did what God told him to? *[He loved and trusted God, he was a good person, obedient, he was afraid...]*

- What did God tell Noah to do when he saw a rainbow?

- How do you think this helped Noah and his family?

- What will you think of next time you see a rainbow?

God's Great Plan

Activities

1. Imagine you are one of Noah's children. He has just told you that the family must get into the ark quickly. Think of some questions you want to ask him. Your teacher can pretend to be Noah and answer them!

2. **Work Book** page 6 'Noah and the Ark'

3. Make a rainbow wrist band that you can wear to remind you of God's promise.
    a) Cut a piece of paper or thin card approximately 18cm in length and 3cm in width. Make a small slit, one on the right and the other on the left at either end.
    b) Children colour their wristband the colours of the rainbow.
    c) They wear it in religious education class or keep it in their workbook.

4. Create a rainbow dance to a song. Children use crepe paper streamers of different colours. To make a streamer, fold half an art straw and tie a crepe paper streamer to it. Choose one of the following songs:
   Who Built the Ark?' Alleluia by A.C. Black
   'Who put the colours in the Rainbow' from 'Come & Sing', Scripture Union

ICT Noah: http://www.refuel.org.uk/projects/ks1_topics/old_testament/old_testament.html
www.reonline.co.uk click on 'Bible', then 'Noah's Ark'.

Mary our Mother

1.2 Mary our Mother

Catechism of the Catholic Church

'God sent forth his Son', but to prepare a body for him, he wanted the free co-operation of a creature. For this, from all eternity God chose for the mother of His Son a daughter of Israel, a young Jewish woman of Nazareth in Galilee, 'a virgin betrothed to a man whose name was Joseph, of the house of David; and the virgin's name was Mary'. (Para. 488)

'In a wholly singular way she co-operated by her obedience, faith, hope and burning charity in the Saviour's work of restoring supernatural life to souls. For this reason she is mother to us in the order of grace.' (Para. 968)

AT1 & AT2
Learning ABOUT and learning FROM the Catholic Faith

Key Learning Objectives
In this unit you will have the opportunity to:

- Know that God sent the Angel Gabriel to ask Mary to be the mother of His son.
  - Reflect on Mary's response.

- Hear about Mary's visit to her cousin, Elizabeth.
  - Reflect on their good news.

- Prepare to celebrate the birth of Jesus.
  - Think of how we can prepare for it.

- Know the story of the birth of Jesus.
  - Be aware that God sent Jesus to help us.

- Know that Mary is our mother too.
  - Think about how Mary looks after us.

Theological Notes

Q. What do we know about God's choice of Mary as mother of His Son?

From the very first moment Mary appears in the New Testament, in the mystery of the Annunciation (Lk. 1:26 ff), she is set forth as the 'model of faith'. It is God who breaks into Mary's life: Mary does not go to God; it is God who comes to Mary, taking the initiative of His saving and redeeming love. Addressed by the archangel Gabriel, in God's name, as "full of grace" or "highly favoured one", Mary is "greatly troubled": there must be some mistake here; she knows herself to be the simple, humble maidservant of the Lord. "Do not be afraid, Mary," she is reassured, as were Moses and the prophets of old, or later the apostles of the new dispensation; "it is **you** who have found favour with the Lord". And when she is further told that she "will conceive and bear a son who will be called the Son of the Most High", she does not jump to appropriate this role, which every young woman in Israel was longing for – to be the mother of the Messiah. In all truth and honesty, Mary seeks to clarify her real situation: "How can this be (that I have a son), since I have no relations with men?" Once again, she is reassured, in God's name, that God and God alone will do it all: "The Holy Spirit will come upon you, and the power of the Most High will overshadow you; therefore, the child that will be born of you will be called Son of God." Even **then**, Mary does not respond, as it were appropriating the gift of the Lord; she does **not** say anything like: "All right, then, I will be the Mother of the Incarnate Lord." Her only response is that of genuine faith, that of total availability to God as God, to God's call and vocation, from her real situation and accepting herself for who she is: "I am the maidservant of the Lord; let it be done to me – not **I** shall do it – according to your Word". With all the power and energy of her free will, **Mary let God be God** in her life; Mary gave God a real, serious chance in her life.

Q. What is Advent?
Advent is the time before Christmas when we prepare to celebrate the coming of Jesus as the fulfilment of our **HOPE:** *"Come, Lord Jesus!"*

We know that Jesus has already come and while we celebrate his birthday, we are *"longing and yearning"* for Jesus Christ who is still to come again at the end of time to bring to a final fulfilment his Father's loving plan of liberation, salvation and redemption. So our **Advent** is a 'remembering' of the *past* coming of Jesus in his incarnation and birth, a time to prepare to celebrate his birthday at Christmas and to 'get ready' for the real *future* coming of him at the end of time.

Q. What is Mary's role in our life?
"Mary is Mother of God and our mother, so we can entrust all our cares and petitions to her" (CCC 2677).

Mary's role in relation to the Church and to all humanity: wholly human as she was, hers was a privileged role because, in the working out of the mystery of redemption, she – in the name of all humanity – said her unconditional 'YES', freely and actively, to God's invitation to collaborate in God's plan for saving us.

Mary our Mother

Mary our Mother

> Know that God sent the Angel Gabriel to ask Mary to be the Mother of His Son.
> Talk about Mary's response to God.

Scripture text and notes for Teachers

The Annunciation
"In the sixth month, the angel Gabriel was sent by God to a town in Galilee called Nazareth, to a virgin betrothed to a man named Joseph, of the House of David; and the virgin's name was Mary. He went in and said to her, 'Rejoice, so highly favoured! The Lord is with you.' She was deeply disturbed by these words and asked herself what this greeting could mean, but the angel said to her, 'Mary, do not be afraid; you have won God's favour. Listen! You are to conceive and bear a son, and you must name him Jesus. He will be great and will be called Son of the Most High. The Lord God will give him the throne of his ancestor David; he will rule over the House of Jacob for ever and his reign will have no end.' Mary said to the angel, 'But how can this come about, since I am a virgin?' 'The Holy Spirit will come upon you', the angel answered, 'and the power of the Most High will cover you with its shadow. And so the child will be holy and will be called Son of God. Know this too: your kinswoman Elizabeth has, in her old age, herself conceived a son, and she whom people called barren is now in her sixth month, for nothing is impossible to God.' 'I am the handmaid of the Lord,' said Mary 'let what you have said be done to me.' And the angel left her." (Lk. 1:26-38)

Notes: Angels are servants and messengers of God. They are part of God's creation. 'Angel' just means 'messenger'.

KEY QUESTIONS (to share with children at any point)

Why do you think God chose Mary?
What do you think Mary thought when the angel asked her to be the Mother of His son?

Introductory Activity
Discuss with children the type of messages that they are asked to take, e.g. take the register; take a written message to the office etc.

Discussion could follow about the importance of being trustworthy when taking messages and delivering them to the right person and of bringing back a reply which is also correct.

Mary our Mother

Link Sentence

Today, we are going to hear how God sent a very important message to someone He had chosen to do a very important job for Him – and what that person decided to do.

Look at picture on page 7 in Big Book: The Annunciation

God wanted Mary to be the Mother of His son.

He sent an angel to ask her.

Mary said YES!

She loved God very much.

Questions on Big Book

- Who do you see in the picture?
- What is Mary doing in the picture? *[Emphasise that Mary was not a rich person with servants, she was probably engaged in some simple domestic task.]*

Text to read to children:

The Angel Gabriel had a very special job to do. He had a message from God for someone. Someone God had chosen a long time ago, someone who had the most important job ever to do for God, if only she would say 'yes'. Her name was Mary and she lived in a little town called Nazareth.

The angel came gently to where Mary lived. 'Hail Mary!' he said to her. [This was how people said hello to each other in those days.] 'You are full of grace', the angel said. [This meant that God had blessed her]. Then the angel said: 'The Lord is with you'. Mary was a bit scared. People don't often see angels and she wondered why he was there.

Mary our Mother

"Don't be afraid, Mary," the angel said. "God has chosen you to be the mother of His son. And his name will be Jesus.

Mary was very surprised at this. "How can this happen?" she said, "I haven't got a husband!" Mary was engaged to a man called Joseph, but they weren't married yet.

"Don't worry," said the angel, "the Holy Spirit will come to you and make this happen."

Mary thought quietly for a moment. She was a bit worried, but she loved and trusted God and wanted to do what He asked. She turned to the angel.

"Yes," she said. "I will do what God wants." And the angel left.

Questions to ask about story:

- How do you think Mary felt when the angel spoke to her? *[Surprise, fear, wonder, perhaps even love.]*

- Have *you* heard the words that the Angel said to Mary? When do we say them? *("Hail Mary, full of grace, the Lord is with you"; from the 'Hail Mary').*

- Why do you think God had chosen Mary? *[She was good, obedient and most important of all she loved and trusted God.]*

- Do you think Mary could have said 'no' when the angel asked her to be the Mother of God's son? *[She could have refused without being in the wrong– emphasise her free choice made because of her love for God.]*

- Have you ever been asked to do something important? What was it? How did you feel?

Activities

1. Make an angel to remind you of the story. [When Christmas gets nearer the angels can form part of the heavenly host with the shepherds.]
   Suggestions for making angels:
   a) Use silver and gold doilies.
   b) Use knitting wool cones or cones of paper for bodies and spheres for heads (available from craft shops).
   c) Use different foils, tissues, glitter etc. to make two dimensional angels to suggest light (coming from heaven).
   d) Use cellophane and transparent materials to make angels on the window.

Mary our Mother

2. **Work Book** page 7 'Mary'

3. **CIRCLE TIME** to thank Mary for saying 'Yes' to God.
   Children to gather round statue or picture of Mary, if possible one where she is not holding baby Jesus. Candles lit.

   Teacher: Mary said yes to God and became the mother of His son Jesus. We are going to thank her for saying yes.

   Children could place their angels, flowers or other offerings round Mary's feet. They can say, 'Thank you, Mary', or other words they have prepared as they do this.

   A song to Mary could be sung, e.g. 'The Angel Gabriel from heaven came', Hymns Old & New.

   Invite the children to join in saying the 'Hail Mary'.
   [Teacher can point out that this is a special prayer because we use the same words as the angel did. We don't have any photographs of Mary, but lots of people have painted picture and made statues of how they think she might have looked. We can use these pictures and statues to look at and help us to think about the real person.]

$. **Work Book** page 8 'Mary & the Angel: Complete the sentences.

5. **Listen** to story 'The Angel Gabriel comes to see Mary'
   Sing song 'An Angel Came from Heaven' from CD
   Stories and Songs of Jesus from Mcrimmons Publishing, 10-12 High Street, Great Wakering, Essex SS3 0EQ, Fax. 01702 216082/

6. **Extension task:** Compare Big Book picture with other famous annunciation pictures to identify what is the same and what is different. Suggest reasons.

Some useful websites:
www.christusrex.org/www2/art/angels.htm
www.hermanoleon.org
www.FaithClipart.com

Mary our Mother

Mary visits Elizabeth

> Hear about Mary's visit to her cousin Elizabeth.
> Reflect on their good news.

Scripture text and notes for Teachers

The Visitation
"Mary set out at that time and went as quickly as she could to a town in the hill country of Judah. She went into Zechariah's house and greeted Elizabeth. Now as soon as Elizabeth heard Mary's greeting, the child leapt in her womb and Elizabeth was filled with the Holy Spirit. She gave a loud cry and said, 'Of all women you are the most blessed, and blessed is the fruit of your womb. Why should I be honoured with a visit from the mother of my Lord? For the moment your greeting reached my ears, the child in my womb leapt for joy. Yes, blessed is she who believed that the promise made her by the Lord would be fulfilled.'"
(Lk. 1:39-45)

Notes: Mary went to see Elizabeth to be of service to her in her need because she was pregnant; so too was Mary. Jesus (in the womb of Mary) sanctified the baby in the womb of Elizabeth (John the Baptist).

Key Questions [To share with children at any point]

Why do you think Mary went to see Elizabeth?
What news did Mary have for Elizabeth?
What do you think she said to her?

Introductory Activity
Sharing news: Encourage the children to share news which was both exciting and a bit scary – e.g. a move to a new house, a new baby in the family, a new school, a visit to a new friend's house, starting school. Bring out the idea that we can be excited and happy about something at the same time as feeling a little nervous and anxious.

Link Sentence
Today, we are going to hear how Mary shared her news with her cousin Elizabeth, and how Elizabeth also had some news to talk about.

Mary our Mother

Look at the picture on page 8 of the Big Book: Mary Visits Elizabeth

Mary went to see her cousin Elizabeth.

Elizabeth was going to have a baby too.

She knew Mary's baby would be very special.

Question to ask on picture in Big Book
- Who can you see in the picture?
- What do you think Mary wanted to tell Elizabeth?

Text to read to children

Do you remember that Mary had a message from the Angel Gabriel? After the angel had gone, Mary was very thoughtful. She sat quite still in her house and thought for a long time about what the angel had said. The angel had told her another piece of news as well. He told her that her cousin Elizabeth was going to have a baby. Everyone knew that Elizabeth was much too old to have babies.

"If Elizabeth is going to have a baby, God must be able to do absolutely anything!" Mary thought to herself. And then she thought how old Elizabeth was and how tired she would be.

"I will go and visit her and stay to help," Mary decided, and she got up quickly and started to pack some things.

It was a long walk over the mountains to where Elizabeth lived with her husband, too far to walk in one day, or even two days. It must have taken Mary three days to walk there and nobody knows who went with her to help her. Perhaps Joseph went with her? But in the end she arrived safely at Elizabeth's house.

Mary our Mother

Elizabeth came out to meet her and shouted with joy to see her.

"Blessed are you among women!" she called, and Mary sang a song of happiness to God.

Elizabeth knew that God had blessed Mary, more than any other woman and she knew that this baby was going to be very special.

Mary stayed there with Elizabeth for about three months, and then she went home. She had things to do. She had to get ready for her own baby to be born, a baby who was the Son of God.

Questions to ask:

- Why do you think Mary went to visit Elizabeth? [*To congratulate her about expecting a baby, to help her.*]

- How do you think Elizabeth felt about having a baby? [*Excited, scared, can't believe she was having a baby at last, full of thanks to God.*]

- Elizabeth said: 'Blessed are you among women". Do you ever say these words? When do you say them?

- What do we learn about Mary from this story?

- Why do you think this story is important for us to know? [*So we understand Mary's kindness and concern for people, so we know she trusted what the angel told her. Some children may recognise Elizabeth's greeting as being part of the 'Hail Mary'*]

- Is anyone here waiting for a new baby in their family? How do you feel about it?

Activities
1. In class or groups, discuss what you think Elizabeth and Mary might have said to each other once they got inside the house and sat down. This could be acted out in pairs.

2. **Work Book** page 9 'Mary goes to see Elizabeth'.

Mary our Mother

Advent

> Know that Advent is a time when we prepare to celebrate the birthday of Jesus.
> Talk about the preparations we can make.

Notes for Teachers

Advent is a time when we prepare to celebrate the coming of our Lord: immediately at Christmas, and at the end of time for Jesus Christ's glorious coming.

Advent is also a time when we train ourselves to be ready to meet Jesus who comes to us every day in persons, events and in situations and lovingly challenges us. We may not be able to see or understand immediately how he is helping us but if we keep our hearts open to him he will give us what is best.

Churches and homes often have an Advent wreath as a focus for the four weeks of Advent. A circle of greenery includes four candles, one to be lit on each of the four Sundays of Advent. Three of the candles are purple and one is rose, the liturgical colour of the third Sunday, or Gaudete Sunday. Gaudete means 'rejoice'.

KEY QUESTIONS (To share with children at any time)

Who is Jesus?
Why do you think we celebrate Jesus' birthday?
What do you think we can do to get ready for his birthday?
What day do we call his birthday?

Introductory Activity
Teacher brings in an Advent wreath and puts the four candles in front of the children.

Teacher explains that four weeks before Christmas we get ready to celebrate the birthday of Jesus.

Link Sentence
Today, we are going to hear how some children came from a different country just in time to see how we prepare for Christmas here.

Mary our Mother

Look at the picture on page 9 of the Big Book: Advent

In Advent we prepare for Jesus' birthday.

We call Jesus' birthday 'Christmas'.

We celebrate with our families.

Question on picture in Big Book
- What can you see in the picture that shows people are getting ready for Christmas? [*Advent wreath and family talking about how to prepare for the birthday of Jesus.*]

- What preparations can we make? [*Putting up the crib, singing carols, doing Nativity play.*]

Text to read to children:
The big aeroplane touched the ground and bounced a little before it came to a stop. Katalin and Vidor were very excited. They could hardly keep still in their seats until it was time to get off. This was their first visit to England and it was almost Christmas time. They couldn't wait to get to their friend Anna's house and start getting ready to celebrate Jesus' birthday.

As the taxi took them through the city, the children noticed all the lights and decorations in the shop windows and when they left the city and drove through quieter streets, they saw that many houses were also decorated.

"Why have the houses got lights on?" Katalin asked her mother. "Is it because the people inside are happy about Christmas?"

Her mother smiled.

Mary our Mother

"I hope so," she said.

At last, they arrived at their friends' house and Vidor and Katalin helped their mother carry the bags inside. Their friends rushed out to help them and there were hugs and kisses all round.

Vidor saw the Christmas tree waiting to be decorated.

"Why do you have a tree indoors?" he asked.

"The tree is still green, even in the middle of the winter," Anna answered. "It reminds us of the new life Jesus came to bring. And we put lights on it to remind us that Jesus is the light of the world."

Katalin saw the Advent calendar and went over to have a look.

"What is this for," she asked, looking at the little pictures of angels, shepherds and stars.

"It's to remind us of all the things that happened when Jesus was born," her mother said, and Katalin thought of the story about Jesus being born in Bethlehem.

Before supper the family gathered round the Advent wreath. They lit the candles and said a prayer together. They promised to try to be extra kind to everyone.

Questions to ask about story:
- What do you do to prepare for Christmas? *[Teacher needs to be aware that children of other faiths may be present.]*

- Let us think about things we can do. *[Teacher needs to encourage children to think beyond presents and decorations and to think of helping, being kind, saying an extra prayer etc.]*

- What happens in school to prepare for Christmas?

- What happens in Church? [Advent wreath, purple vestments – some children may be able to name these.]

Mary our Mother

Activities

1. **Work Book** page 10 'Advent Promises'.

2. Each child makes an Advent candle with a flame *(Card for candle and shiny paper for flame)*. Write an Advent promise on a piece of paper and stick it onto the candle. Use candles for display.

3. Have a weekly Advent prayer circle.
   Sit in circle and each child says how s/he will prepare for the birthday of Jesus that week. Sing/listen to song.
   Advent wreath is in the centre of the circle and as each candle is lit they could say the following prayer either with or after the teacher. This could be repeated each week.

   God our Father, we ask you to bless our plans for Advent. Help us to prepare well for the birth of your son Jesus, so that when Christmas comes we can celebrate with Mary and all your friends. Amen.

4. Make an Advent display. Cover a display board with coloured paper. Make four 'windows' by stapling squares of contrasting coloured paper to make a little 'shutter' on each window. Staple one side of the shutter and keep it closed with blue tack. Decorate windows with candles. Underneath put pictures of people, symbols etc. linked to Advent. Each week open a window to remind the children that the time is getting closer for the birth of Jesus.

5. Have a small crib with a prayer card. Each child has the opportunity to take it home one evening during Advent as a special treat.

6. **ICT for children:** www.request.org.uk Select 'Infants' then 'Festivals' then 'Christmas' and do one of the activities.

Mary our Mother

Birth of Jesus

> Know about the journey to Bethlehem and the birth of Jesus.
> Think about what happened.

Scripture text for Teachers

The Birth of Jesus
"Now at this time Caesar Augustus issued a decree for a census of the whole world to be taken. This census – the first – took place while Quirinius was governor of Syria, and everyone went to his own town to be registered. So Joseph set out from the town of Nazareth in Galilee and travelled up to Judaea, to the town of David called Bethlehem, since he was of David's House and line, in order to be registered together with Mary, his betrothed, who was with child. While they were there the time came for her to have her child, and she gave birth to a son, her first-born." (Lk. 2:1-7)

Key Questions (To share with the children at any point)

How do you think people travelled long ago?
How do you think Mary and Joseph went to Bethlehem?
Where do you think they wanted to stay?

Introductory Activity
a) Discuss what a new baby needs, focus on helplessness and need to prepare for a baby.
Children to consider the needs of a new-born baby by making a collection of items, or pictures of items that a baby is considered to need today.
Items could be brought from home to display, or drawn.

b) Teacher has a selection of pictures of things for a new baby.
Discuss what these things are for and why we need them.

c) Where do you think would be a good place for the baby to be born? Why?

d) What would you put in the room? Why?

Link Sentence
Today, we are going to hear how Mary and Joseph travelled to Bethlehem and the problem they had trying to find a place to stay.

Mary our Mother

Look at the picture on page 10 in Big Book: Journey to Bethlehem

Mary and Joseph had to go to Bethlehem.

It was a long journey.

They could not find a place to stay.

Questions to ask on picture in Big Book
- Who can you see in the picture?

- Where are they going?

Text to read to children:

It was almost time for Mary's baby to be born. Joseph and Mary had to go to Bethlehem, the town where Joseph had been born. The emperor said everyone had to be counted. So they just had to go.

It was a long way to Bethlehem. It took them at least three days to get there and Mary was very, very tired. Joseph began to look for somewhere for them to stay, but lots of other people had come to Bethlehem as well. It was only a little town and everywhere was full up.

Mary and Joseph must have thought they would have nowhere to stay that night, but at last they found a little space in a stable where animals lived.
They were so tired, they were happy to stay there. Joseph tried to make a comfortable place for Mary.

That night, Mary's baby was born. Mary wrapped him up in the clothes she had ready with her, but she hadn't been able to bring a cradle all the way from Nazareth. She looked round for somewhere to lay her little baby down to sleep. Then she saw the manger, where the hay was put for the animals to eat. It looked warm and soft, so Mary laid baby Jesus gently down inside.

Mary our Mother

Questions to ask about story:

- How do you think Mary felt when they got to Bethlehem and there was nowhere for them to stay?

- What kind of place would you have chosen for the son of God to be born? [*Children may say a palace, a 'posh' house, somewhere important.*] Why?

Activities

1. Hot seat Mary: Children take turns to be Mary and the others ask questions, for example:
   - What was the journey to Bethlehem like?
   - Where did they stay?
   - What happened?

2. Write a sentence to thank God for Mary's baby.
   Children share their prayer in a 'circle time'.
   At the end of the 'circle time' prayers could be put in a basket and placed by the crib.

3. **Listen** to the story 'The Story of How Jesus Was Born' and **song 'Glory to God'**. CD Stories and Songs of Jesus

4. Song: 'No Room at the Inn', Out of the Ark Music, Songs for every Christmas by Mark & Helen Johnson.

ICT http://ngfl.northumberland.gov.uk/christmas/nativity/nativity.html

Mary our Mother

Visit of the Shepherds

> Know that the shepherds were first to hear about the birth of Jesus.
> Reflect on the joy of Mary and Joseph.

Scripture text for Teachers

When Jesus was born in the stable in Bethlehem, Mary "wrapped him in swaddling clothes, and laid him in a manger because there was no room for them at the inn. In the countryside close by there were shepherds who lived in the fields and took it in turns to watch their flocks during the night. The angel of the Lord appeared to them and the glory of the Lord shone round them. They were terrified, but the angel said, 'Do not be afraid. Listen, I bring you news of great joy, a joy to be shared by the whole people. Today, in the town of David a saviour has been born to you; he is Christ the Lord. And here is a sign for you: you will find a baby wrapped in swaddling clothes and lying in a manger.' And suddenly with the angel there was a great throng of the heavenly host, praising God and singing:

'Glory to God in the highest heaven,
And peace to men who enjoy his favour'.

Now when the angels had gone from them into heaven, the shepherds said to one another, 'Let us go to Bethlehem and see this thing that has happened which the Lord has made known to us'. So they hurried away and found Mary and Joseph, and the baby lying in the manger. When they saw the child they repeated what they had been told about him, and everyone who heard it was astonished at what the shepherds had to say. As for Mary, she treasured all things and pondered them in her heart. And the shepherds went back glorifying and praising God for all they had heard and seen; it was exactly as they had been told." (Lk. 2: 7-20)

KEY QUESTIONS (to share with children at any point)

What do you think happened when Jesus was born?
What do you think Mary thought about it?
How do you think Joseph was feeling?
Who heard the news first?
How did the shepherds find out?

Introductory Activity
About hearing good news.
When did you hear it?
Who told you?
How did you feel?
Who did you tell?

Mary our Mother

Link sentence
Now we are going to find out how the good news of the birth of Jesus spread.

Look at picture on page 11 in the Big Book:
The shepherds visit Jesus

Baby Jesus was born.

Mary and Joseph were delighted.

The shepherds arrived.

They loved baby Jesus very much.

Questions to ask about the Big Book Picture
- What do you see in the picture?

- What do you think Mary and Joseph were saying to each other?

- What did they say to baby Jesus?

- Who were the first people to find out about the birth of Jesus?

Text to read to children
On the hills outside Bethlehem, there were some shepherds. It was their job to look after the sheep and keep them safe. They were huddled up together, keeping warm, when suddenly they saw a great light in the sky. It was an angel, sent from God! The shepherds were very frightened, but the angel said, "Don't be afraid! I'm bringing you some wonderful news. News which will make everyone happy! Tonight, **the Son of God has been born**. You will find him all wrapped up and lying in a manger." Then, as they watched, the shepherds saw more and more and more angels till the whole sky was full of them, all shining and singing. It must have been a wonderful sight.

When the angels had gone, the shepherds said to themselves, "Let's go to Bethlehem and see this for ourselves." So they hurried off and went to Bethlehem, and when they got there they found everything exactly as the angel had told them – Mary and Joseph and baby Jesus lying in the manger.

Mary our Mother

The shepherds told everyone they met what had happened, and of course, Mary remembered everything that happened on that first Christmas night.

Questions to ask about the story

- What do you think Mary thought about the angel coming to the shepherds?

- What do you think the shepherds said to the people they met on the way back from the stable?

- If you had visited Jesus in the stable what would you have taken as a gift?

- Why do you think God chose poor shepherds to be his first visitors? [*Encourage children to understand that Jesus came for everyone, even the poorest and the least important. It was not that God preferred the poor, but that they were open to him.*]

Activities

1. Imagine you are one of the shepherds and you are telling someone what happened to you that night. What do you think is the most important part of the story you have to tell? Make a picture and call it "The shepherd's story." It can be part of a display. Those children who are able can write or dictate why they chose that part of the story.

2. Have a collection of printed Christmas cards in a variety of styles which show the shepherds or the angels or the stable at Bethlehem. Discuss with children why the artist chose to depict the scene in the way s/he did. Ask children what aspect of the story they would choose for a card, and why. Discuss the wording inside. Children can then design their own cards.

3. Children take turns to be shepherds on the hillside for 'Hot Seating'
   Some prompt questions:
   - How did you feel when you saw the angels?
   - What did the angels tell you to do?
   - How did you get to the stable?
   - What was it like when you saw baby Jesus?
   - When you left the stable, what did you do?

4. **Work Book** page 11 'The Shepherds'

5. **Work Book** page 12 'The Shepherds hurry away'.

6. **Teacher's Book** page 48 'Christmas Day' to be used for discussion.

7. Role-play the conversation between Mary and Joseph when the shepherds left.

8. **ICT for children** www.reonline.co.uk select 'Infants' and click on 'Festivals' to listen to Christmas Story.
   http://www.ngfl-cymru.org.uk/vtc/ngfl/re/b-dag/ngfl-container/re-unit1-en.html

Mary our Mother

Mary is our Mother

> Know that Mary is our Mother too.
> Think about how she looks after us.

Notes for the Teachers

Mary's role in relation to the Church and to all humanity: wholly human as she was, hers was a privileged role because, in the working out of the mystery of redemption, she – in the name of all humanity – said her unconditional 'YES', freely and actively, to God's invitation to collaborate in God's plan for saving us.

KEY QUESTIONS (To share with children at any point)

Why do you think Mary looks after us?
How do you think she does this?

Introductory Activity
Involve the children in thinking about how mothers love and care for their children. Write their responses on the board.

Link Sentence
Today, we are going to hear how a little boy called Jack asked Mary our Mother in heaven, for help.

Look at the picture on page 12 in the Big Book: Jack's Mother

Jack felt a bit sad.

He didn't feel like smiling.

He asked Mary, our Mother in heaven, to help.

Soon he was smiling again. He knew Mary would help them.

45

Mary our Mother

Question to ask on picture in Big Book
- What do you see in the picture?

Text to read to children:

Jack was feeling a bit sad. His Mum was not very well. She had been in hospital for a long time and Jack missed having her at home.

There was something else worrying Jack. When he went to visit his mum in hospital, he always had a sad face. He tried really hard, but he just couldn't smile. This made his mum sad too. Every day Jack tried again, but it was no use. He just couldn't do it.

"Cheer up, Jack," the nurse said. "We're taking good care of your mum in here, you know."

And Jack knew they were, but he still couldn't smile, even to make his mum feel better.

One day, Jack went to see his mum as usual and he climbed up on to the bed to sit next to her. He looked at the picture of Mary that hung above the bed. His mum saw him looking at it.

"Did you know, Jack", she said quietly, "you have two mothers really? One of them is me, right here next to you, but the other one is Mary in heaven."

Jack thought about this. His mother gave him a hug.

"Why don't you ask Mary our Mother to help you when you feel sad and lonely?" she said. "Mothers always want to help."

Jack knew this was true and he looked up at the picture again. He didn't say anything, but in his heart he asked Mary to help him. When he got home and went to bed, he remembered the picture of Mary. He closed his eyes and said a prayer in his heart.

The next day, when Jack went to visit his mum in hospital, the first thing he saw was the picture of Mary above the bed. Slowly, a big smile spread across his face and he gave his mum a big hug as a present. You can guess how much better that made his mum feel.

Questions to ask about story:

- Why do you think Jack felt so sad? [*Not only missed his Mum but missed her care for him.*]

Mary our Mother

- Why couldn't Jack smile when he went to visit his mum? [*Too sad, worried, some children may be able to say that he perhaps didn't feel he should be smiling in a sad situation.*]

- Why did Jack ask Mary to help him? [*His mother suggested it, Mary is his/our Mother in heaven and we can ask her for help, he wanted help, he wanted something that was good.*]

- What do you think Jack might have said to Mary in his heart? [*Encourage replies which make it clear that Mary loves us and prays for us.*]

- Why do you think Jack wanted to give his mum a smile as a present?

- Do you ever ask Mary our Mother in heaven to pray for you, or help you? [*Encourage awareness of situations where a mother's help is appropriate, e.g. anything which encourages the child to think of others first, or of the right course of action.*]

Activities

1. **Work Book** page 13 'Mary our Mother'. Write two prayers to Mary.

2. As a class or group, make an acrostic using either MARY or MOTHER to suggest some motherly qualities. Children could then copy this and decorate it.

   e.g. Mother of Jesus and my mother

   Always looking after me

   Ready to help me

   Your mother too.

   OR Make a List Poem adding words and pictures
   Mary is ....
   Mary is ....
   Mary is ....

   (happy good special my mother helps me)

3. Display a large print copy of the 'Hail Mary'; you could put the three different parts in different fonts or colours. Read it slowly to the children, pausing at the end of the first two sections to see if they remember who first said that part. (The Angel Gabriel, Elizabeth) Read the third part and explain that the Church has added that part for us to say. You may want to explain the unfamiliar words such as thee, thy, thou, grace, blessed, fruit of thy womb; or just respond if there is a question on them. See 'Hail Mary' page 49.

Christmas Day

What do you see in this picture?

If you were there what would you do?

What would you bring?

What might Mary be thinking?

How do you think Joseph is feeling?

Hail Mary

Hail Mary, full of grace, the Lord is with thee. Blessed art thou among women,
and blessed is the fruit of thy womb, Jesus.

Holy Mary, Mother of God, pray for us sinners, now, and at the hour of our death. Amen.

Families and Celebrations

1.3 Families & Celebrations

Religious Education Curriculum Directory
"Foundations for love of neighbour, together with Christian values which promote respect for authority and citizenship, are laid in family life. The values of family life are a vital element in the social doctrine of the Church." p. 35

"The Church is the family of God, the People that God gathers in the whole world." p. 19

"In Baptism we are reborn as children of God in Christ and enlightened by the Holy Spirit." p. 24

AT1 & AT2
Learning ABOUT and learning FROM the Catholic Faith

Key Learning Objectives
In this unit you will have the opportunity to:

- Know that we all belong to a family.
   - Think about how we can love and help each other.

- Know that Mary and Joseph took Jesus to the Temple as a baby.
   - Think about why this was a very special occasion.

- Know that Jesus belonged to a family.
   - Think of things he may have done with his family.

- Know about the loss and finding of Jesus.
   - Reflect on the feelings of Mary and Joseph when Jesus was lost and then found.

- Begin to understand what it means to belong to our Church family.
   - Reflect on what we do together.

- Know that we become a member of the Church by receiving the Sacrament of Baptism.
   - Talk about what happens when a baby is baptised.

Theological Notes

Q. What does the presentation of Jesus in the Temple mean?
"The presentation of Jesus in the temple shows him to be the firstborn Son who belongs to the Lord. With Simeon and Anna, all Israel awaits its encounter with the Saviour..... Jesus is recognized as the long-expected Messiah, the 'light to the nations' and the 'glory of Israel', but also 'a sign that is spoken against'. The sword of sorrow predicted for Mary announces Christ's perfect and unique oblation (offering) on the cross that will impart the salvation God had 'prepared in the presence of all peoples'." CCC 529

In this 'external' observance, both Jesus and Mary were 'interiorly' (in their hearts) repeating and deepening their self-offering and self-gift to God the Father's holy will (**Jesus** - Hebrews 10:5-10; **Mary** - Luke 1:28).

Simeon and Anna (Luke 2:22-38) had 'open hearts'; they were led by the Spirit of God and recognised in Jesus the Saviour of the world (the 'light of the world').

Q. What do we know about the early life of Jesus?
"During the greater part of his life, Jesus shared the condition of the vast majority of human beings: a daily life spent without evident greatness, a life of manual labour. His religious life was that of a Jew obedient to the law of God, a life in the community." CCC531.

When Jesus was twelve years old (and we know that in the Jewish law, a Jewish boy becomes an adult at the age of twelve, becoming as he does bar-mitzvah, son of the law), he was lost in the temple, and his mother and foster father found him there after looking for him over three days of great anguish and sorrow. We recall that his mother said to him: "Why have you done such a thing to us? We have been looking for you with hearts full of sorrow and anxiety." What was Jesus' response? With calm intransigence he replied: "How is it you looked for me? Did you not know that I must be about my Father's business? Did you not know that I must be in the house of my Father and the things that concern my Father?" Already at the age of twelve, his life-orientation was clear. His identity was clear: he lived **only** for his Father. He was inviting his mother and foster-father to this freedom for the Father **alone.**

Q. Why is the family important?
"The family is the community in which, from childhood, one can learn moral values, begin to honour God, and make good use of freedom. Family life is an initiation into life in society" CCC 2207. Family bonds are important, and as such, are to be nurtured, but with sensitivity to the fact that many families are wounded or broken. As Catholic Christians, we become part of the universal family of the Church at our Baptism.

Q. What happens at Baptism?
"In Baptism we are reborn as children of God in Jesus Christ and enlightened by the Holy Spirit." In brief, we enter into the life of Jesus and receive his Spirit. We are cleansed of original sin. We become members of the Church.

Families and Celebrations

Families & Celebrations

> Know that we all belong to a family.
> Think about how we can love and help each other.

Notes for Teachers

There are different patterns for families throughout the world.
We all belong to a family group and some members of the group usually live with us.

When a member of the family does something wrong, he/she is still loved; each person is accepted and loved the way that person is, with all his/her limitations and weaknesses. We call Jesus' family the 'Holy Family'.

Key Questions (To share with children at any point)
How do members of a family show they love one another?
When do we celebrate in the family?

Introductory Activity

Use 'Family scenes' in Work Book page 14 as a stimulus for discussion on different types of families.

Link Sentence
Today, we are going to think about what it means to belong to a family...

Look at the picture on page 13 of Big Book: Families & Celebrations

Families belong together.

They share meals and have fun together.

Families and Celebrations

Questions to ask about picture in Big Book
- What is this family doing?

- Why do you think they have joined their hands?

- Why do you think they want to pray before they eat?

- What is your favourite time with your family?

- What do you like doing best with your family?

Text to read to children

Ida was very excited because it was her birthday. She was six years old and was going to have a party that afternoon.

She watched her mum preparing the food in the kitchen and she asked if she could help to set the table. Her mum said, "Yes, please". Her mum brought in a large birthday cake with six candles ready to be lit.

Mum looked at Ida and said, "You have really made the party table look lovely. Well done." Ida felt very happy.

Mum put some presents on a small table. Ida looked at them and saw that there was one from her granny. She was very excited because it was tied up with shiny ribbon. She said, "Mum, may I open the present from granny. She told me she was going to send me a new dress that she has made for me."

"No, let's wait until the party", said mum.

Ida looked and looked at granny's parcel with the shiny ribbon. Mum left the room. Ida walked over to the parcels and lifted up the one from granny. It looked too small to be the dress her granny had promised her. She tried to guess what was inside. She knew her granny would keep her promise to her, but this present did not feel like a dress.

Ida pulled a bit off the shiny ribbon and then she tried to have a peep. She couldn't quite see inside the parcel, so she pulled off another bit and it all came off and the parcel was open! Inside was a new... story book! Ida looked at the book. It was good but it was not a new dress! She felt very sad because she wanted a dress.

When mum saw what she had done she said, "Oh Ida, I did ask you NOT to open the parcel yet and you DID!" Ida felt very sorry. She knew she should have done as mummy asked. "I'm really sorry", she said. And mum gave her a big hug.

When granny arrived she had a big surprise - the new dress!

Families and Celebrations

Questions to ask about story

- How do people in the story show their love for one another? *(Try to draw out the following: mummy gives birthday party; Ida offers help; some give presents; Ida was sorry when mummy was upset.)*

- How do you think Ida felt at the end of the story?

- What did Ida's Mum say to make her feel better?

Activities

1. **Work Book page 14:** Draw a picture of your own family. Write what you like to do with your family.

2. Explain that we all belong to a family group and that part of that group live with us.

    Children make a stand up figure of one person who cares for them. They use this figure as a puppet to talk about how that person helps them.

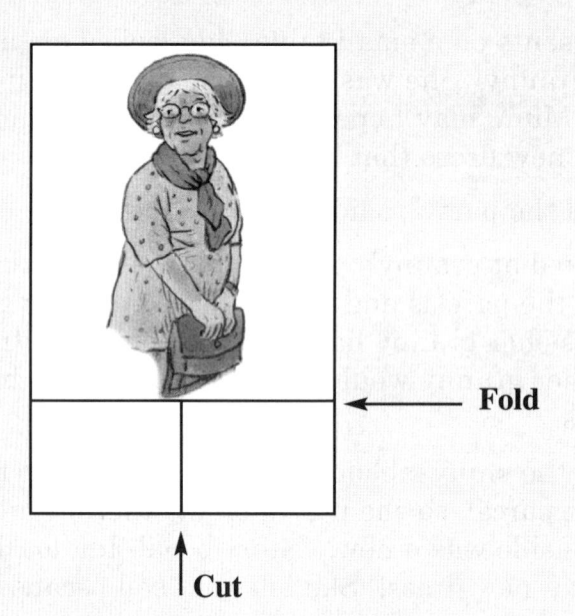

    ← Fold

    ↑ Cut

3. **ICT for children:** www.dottieandbuzz.co.uk click on 'Belonging' and /or 'Forgiving' you will find a variety of activities.

4. Watch the Power Point Presentation on Families & Celebrations.

    For details: email info@tere.org.

Families and Celebrations

The Presentation

> Know that Mary and Joseph took Jesus to the Temple as a baby.
> Think about why this was a very special occasion.

Scripture text for Teachers

We are now going back to the time when Jesus was a baby.
"When the time came for them to be purified as laid down by the Law of Moses, they took Jesus up to Jerusalem to present him to the Lord, observing what stands written in the Law of the Lord: Every first-born male must be consecrated to the Lord – and also to offer in sacrifice, in accordance with what is said in the Law of the Lord, a pair of turtledoves or two young pigeons. Now in Jerusalem there was a man named Simeon. He was an upright and devout man; he looked forward to Israel's comforting and the Holy Spirit rested on him. It had been revealed to him by the Holy Spirit that he would not see death until he had set eyes on the Christ of the Lord. Prompted by the Spirit he came to the Temple; and when the parents brought in the child Jesus to do for him what the Law required, he took him into his arms and blessed God; and he said:
'Now, Master, you can let your servant go in peace,
Just as you promised;
because my eyes have seen the salvation
which you have prepared for all the nations to see,
a light to enlighten the pagans
and the glory of your people Israel'. (Lk. 2:22-32)
The feast of the Presentation is 22nd February.

KEY QUESTIONS (To share with the children at any point)

Why do you think Mary and Joseph took baby Jesus to the Temple?

Who did they meet in the Temple?

What happened?

Introductory Activity

Think of a time when you were taken somewhere special with your family. Who would like to tell us about it?

Link Sentence

We are going to find out why Mary and Joseph took Jesus when he was a baby to a special place and what happened when they got there.

Families and Celebrations

Look at the picture on page 15 of Big Book: The Presentation

Mary and Joseph took Jesus to the Temple.

They wanted to thank God for their beautiful baby.

They met Simeon and Anna. They believed that Jesus was the king of the world.

Question on the picture in the Big Book
- Who do you see in the picture?
- Why are they there?
- Why do you think Simeon and Anna are looking so happy?

Text to read to children

A long time ago when Jesus was still a baby, Mary and Joseph took him to the Temple in Jerusalem. This is where people went to worship God.

"It is time to thank God for our baby", they said to one another.

On the day of their visit, an old man called Simeon was in the Temple. For many years Simeon had been praying that God would keep His promise and send a king to rule over His people.

When Mary and Joseph walked past Simeon, he felt his heart jump inside him. He got up, looked at the baby and straight away he knew this baby was God's special gift for everyone. He was very happy. Simeon asked Mary if he could hold the baby. He took Jesus in his arms and said: "Lord God, you have kept your promise. I can now die a happy man because I have seen Jesus, the light of the world".

Mary and Joseph were amazed at what Simeon said about Jesus and they were even more surprised when an old lady called Anna joined in with him. Anna was well known in the Temple; she was always there praying to God. Anna began to tell everyone that Jesus was the one they had all been waiting for, for a long time. He had come at last!

Families and Celebrations

Questions to ask on story:
- Why did Mary and Joseph go to the Temple with Jesus?
- What happened when they arrived?
- How do you think Simeon was feeling? Why?
- What did Simeon say?
- What do you think Mary was thinking? Why?
- What did Anna do after she had seen Jesus?

Activities

1. Narrate the story again while a small group of children act it out. Have some children acting the part of other parents with their child there in the Temple before Mary and Joseph bring Jesus to Simeon.

2. a) Place children in a circle and have a large candle in the centre.
   b) Light the candle and ask the children to think of the times when they see candles lit. *(birthdays, Christmas, Easter candle, in Church).*
   c) Explain that candles are usually lit for a special time, a celebration. Tell them that, in church for the Feast of the Presentation of the Lord, the congregation hold lighted candles to remind them of the special time when Mary and Joseph brought Jesus to the Temple.
   d) Sing: 'The Light of Christ' or 'Jesus bids us shine' or similar song about 'light' and finish with the Sign of the Cross.

3. **Work Book** page 15 'Jesus is taken to the Temple'.

4. Children sit in a circle.
   Children bring the different items below to place in the centre while the reflection is read by the teacher.
   - Silver cloth and silver moon shape (use silver and gold card for sun & moon shapes)
   - Gold cloth and gold sun shape
   - Candle (lit by an adult on a tray with some damp sand)

Reflection:
The moon gives a silver light at night.
The sun gives a golden light by day.
Jesus is the light of the world day and night.
He is always there, showing us the light of God's love
and making the world a brighter place.

Activity continued on next page

Families and Celebrations

5. Have ready a shape of candle and flame which can be freely decorated by the children – an effective way is to present wax crayons for the children to make designs on the shape of the candle and to wash over this with water-based paint. This can be further decorated with shiny shapes. The candles can be put on display with the title, "Jesus is the Light of the World."

6. **Power Point presentation** 'Presentation in the Temple' for details email: info@tere.org

7. Simeon said that Jesus is the light of the world. Think of how we can show the light of Jesus' love to everyone.

   Design a badge with a smiling face to show that you want to make the world a brighter place.

ICT for children: www.reonline.co.uk click on 'Symbols' for Jesus is the light of the world.

Jesus and his Family

**Know that Jesus belonged to a family.
Think about the things he may have done with his family.**

Notes for Teachers

Although it is tempting to think of Jesus playing with brothers and sisters, the constant Tradition of the Church is that Mary is 'ever-virgin', that is, she remained a virgin and had no more children.

Explain that we sometimes call Jesus, Mary and Joseph 'The Holy Family'.

Key Questions (To share with children at any point)

What do you think Jesus was like when he was little?

What do you think Jesus did when he was with his family?

Introductory Activity

What are some of the things you do with your family.

Families and Celebrations

Look at the picture on page 14 in Big Book: Jesus and his Family

Jesus lived in Nazareth with Mary and Joseph.

Joseph was a carpenter.

Perhaps he let Jesus help him.

Perhaps he showed Jesus how to work with wood.

Questions to ask about the picture:
- Who can you see in the picture?

- What are they doing?

- Name some things you can see in the picture.

- How do you think Jesus helped Joseph in the workshop?

Text to read to children

Jesus grew up in a little town called Nazareth with Mary and Joseph. He was strong and good and he loved God. Joseph worked as a carpenter. He might have had a little workshop next to the house. When Jesus was older, Joseph probably let Jesus help him in the shop. Perhaps he taught him how to use the tools and make things out of wood.

Mary was always busy around the house. Jesus probably helped her with the sweeping and tidying. He would have enjoyed going to the well with Mary to fetch water for cooking and washing. He would have played with the other boys and girls of Nazareth. Mary taught Jesus to pray to God our Father. She would have told him stories from the Holy Scriptures. Jesus must have been very happy living with Mary and Joseph.

Families and Celebrations

Questions to ask on the story
- What was Joseph's job?

- What kinds of things do you think a carpenter could make? (*Cupboards for kitchens, door frames for houses, tables, etc.*)

- What do we have in the classroom that is made of wood?

- What games do you think Jesus would have played with the other children? (*Remember no electricity, no motorised vehicles, warm climate, rural environment*).

- What stories do you think Jesus would have learnt from Mary? (*Guide children to stories they may know from the Old Testament*).

Activities

1. Imagine Mary was out. When she came home and she was putting Jesus to bed, he told her about his day.
   a) What do you think he said?
   b) Role-play the conversation between Mary and Jesus.
   c) Write what Jesus said.

2. **Work Book** page 16 Jesus with his Family

3. Use wood to create something, e.g. a box, a table or a picture frame (for a family photo).

Families and Celebrations

Jesus in the Temple

> Know about the loss and finding of Jesus.
> Reflect on the feelings of Mary and Joseph when Jesus was lost and then found.

Scripture text for Teachers

"Every year his parents used to go to Jerusalem for the feast of the Passover. When Jesus was twelve years old, they went up for the feast as usual. When they were on their way home after the feast, the boy Jesus stayed behind in Jerusalem without his parents knowing it. They assumed he was with the caravan, and it was only after a day's journey that they went to look for him among their relations and acquaintances. When they failed to find him they went back to Jerusalem looking for him everywhere.
Three days later, they found him in the Temple, sitting among the doctors (of the Law), listening to them, and asking them questions; and all those who heard him were astounded at his intelligence and his replies. They were overcome when they saw him, and his mother said to him, 'My child, why have you done this to us? See how worried your father and I have been, looking for you.' 'Why were you looking for me?' he replied. 'Did you not know that I must be busy with my Father's affairs?' But they did not understand what he meant." (Lk. 2: 41-50)

Key Questions (To share with the children at any point).

How do you think Mary felt when she discovered that Jesus was missing?

What did Mary and Joseph do?

Where did they find Jesus?

Introductory Activity
Have you ever got lost?
How did you feel?
How did your parents feel when you were lost?

Role-play with puppets a child getting lost and the parents searching for him/her.

Families and Celebrations

Look at page 16 in Big Book: Jesus in the Temple

> Mary and Joseph thought Jesus was lost.
>
> They were worried and looked for him everywhere.
>
> When they found him, he was talking to the teachers!
>
> Mary and Joseph were so happy to find him.

Questions to ask on the picture in the Big Book:

- Who do you see in the picture?
- What is Jesus doing?
- Who is he with?
- How do you think Mary and Joseph felt when he was lost?
- How do you think they feel now?

Text to read to children:

When Jesus was twelve years old - almost grown up! - the Holy Family went to Jerusalem to celebrate an important feast, as they did every year. At the end of the feast, Mary and Joseph and their friends started off on the long journey back home to Nazareth. Lots of people were with them and they thought Jesus was there too. But at the end of the day, when they stopped to rest for the night, they looked for him - and he wasn't there! He must have stayed behind in Jerusalem, they thought.

Straight away, Mary and Joseph turned back to Jerusalem. How tired they must have been! But they just had to find Jesus.

Jerusalem was a big town and Mary and Joseph searched for three whole days before they found Jesus. Can you guess where they found him? [*Children could make suggestions here.*]

Families and Celebrations

Jesus was in the Temple! He wasn't lost or afraid. He was talking to the teachers who came to the Temple. Of course, the teachers didn't know who Jesus was, so they were very surprised to hear his wise answers to their questions about God. They didn't know that he is the Son of God, but they certainly wondered who he was!

Mary and Joseph were so pleased to see him - they thought he was lost.
"Why did you do this?" Mary asked. "We've been so worried!"

"Why were you looking for me?" Jesus asked. "Didn't you know I had to start doing God's work?"

Mary and Joseph didn't really understand what he meant, but they were so pleased to find him that it didn't matter. Jesus went back home to Nazareth with them and was happy to do everything they said. But Mary often thought of that time and remembered what Jesus had said.

Questions to ask on story:

- Do you remember the first time Mary and Joseph took Jesus to the Temple in Jerusalem? [*Make link here with the Presentation.*]

- How do you think Mary and Joseph felt when they discovered Jesus was not there at the end of the day's travel? [*Point out this was foot travel, took a long time; they might have felt guilty - they had a special child to look after; frightened, very tired but had to go back and look for him.*]

- Where do you think they looked for Jesus before they thought of the Temple? [*Shops, playing with other children, lying hurt somewhere.*]

- Why do you think they were so worried? [*They had been given a special job to do; Jesus was still quite young, though considered almost a man in those times; they were afraid he had been hurt; they were worried that he might be hungry after three days; he had been lost for a long time.*]

- Why do you think Jesus was surprised that they had been searching for him? [*He thought they would think of the Temple (God's house) first; he thought they would understand about doing God's work.*]

Activities

1. a) Role-play Mary and Joseph talking to each other when they discovered that Jesus was lost.

   b) Write down how they felt.

2. **Work Book** page 17 'Jesus is found in the Temple'.

Families and Celebrations

Our Church Family

> Begin to understand what it means to belong to our Church family.
> Reflect on what we do together in church.

Notes for Teachers

We go to church to praise and thank God.
When we go to church it is like going to our shared home.

The Eucharist is our great 'family' (God's family) prayer of thanksgiving and commitment to doing and living today what Jesus did for us, that is, handing himself over in love. We recall that Jesus said: 'Do this in remembrance of me'.

KEY QUESTIONS

Why do you think people go to church?

What do you think happens in church?

Introductory Activity

Have a cluster of night lights in a glass bowl of water. Invite all the children to sit in a circle around it. Have a large picture of Jesus with children (e.g. *Vogel 'Let the Children Come to Me)* where they can all see it.

Together listen or sing 'Listen to Jesus' from 'Share the Light' by Bernadette Farrell.

Link Sentence

Sometimes people sing the song 'Listen to Jesus' in church.

Let us find out why people go to church and what happens there.

Look at the picture on page 17 in the Big Book: **Our Church Family**

Families and Celebrations

Questions to ask on picture in Big Book

> God's people come to church.
> He blesses His people when they come.
>
> We come to be with God, to listen, to talk and to thank Him.

- What do you see in the picture?
- What day do you think it is?
- Why are people here?

Text to read to Children

It's Sunday morning in Tom's house.

Sunday mornings are special because the whole family are up and having breakfast together. Tom was wearing his new shirt and he felt very smart.

Soon it was time to get into the car to go to church. As they went into the church, they saw granny and grandad already there and they went to sit with them. Tom saw his best friend with his family and he wanted to show them his new shirt, but his mum said to wait until afterwards. Tom looked around and saw lots of people he knew.

The priest came in and the Mass began with one of Tom's favourite hymns. They all made the sign of the cross and said sorry to God for anything wrong they had done in the week. Then they all listened to the word of God. Tom liked singing the Alleluia before the Gospel - he knew this was because the Gospel has the words of Jesus himself. They all sat down while Father explained some of the things they had heard from the Bible.

Then everyone stood up to join in saying together what they believe - Tom could join in with the first part now and felt very pleased. Next there were some prayers for people who needed them, and then Tom was asked to help carry the gifts of bread and wine to the altar for the Offertory. He felt a bit nervous, but he had done it once before and he knew he could manage if he walked slowly.

After this, it was the most solemn part of the Mass. Everyone knelt down while the

Families and Celebrations

priest offered the gifts to God the Father. Tom knew that something very important happened at this time. He knew that Jesus came to be with them. He knelt very quietly and prayed to Jesus in his heart.

When the Mass ended, Tom's family all left together saying goodbye to the priest. Tom felt happy and peaceful inside. They chatted to their friends and granny and granddad came home with them for lunch. Tom loved Sundays – Sundays are great!

Questions on story

- When have you been inside a church?
- What was happening?
- What did you do?
- Do you think Tom liked Sundays? Why?
- What was happening in the story to make this day different from other days?
- Would anyone like to tell us what it is like when they go to church?
- What do you like about Sundays?

Activities

1. **If possible**, take children to the church at a quiet time. Show them the font, the altar and the candles. *[It is not necessary at this stage to explain the significance of what they see.]*

   Encourage children to take photos of what they see in church or make observational drawings.

2. **Work Book**: page 18 'A Visit to Church'.

3. Make a point of having a lighted candle (or candles) when prayers are said during the school day. Appoint different children each week to hold the candle unlit and place it in the sand tray for the teacher to light.

4. Learn to sing: 'Listen to Jesus' or 'There is someone who loves me' by Bernadette Farrell – CD 'Share the Light'
   Available from www.viewpoint24.co.uk or
   Viewpoint Direct Resources, Fax. 020 8692 0375

ICT for children www.reonline.co.uk click on 'Church' to write a prayer and print it.

www.request.org.uk Select 'Infants' select 'Going to church'.

Families and Celebrations

Baptism

> Know that we become a member of the Church by being baptised.
> Reflect on what it means to be baptised.

Notes for Teachers

We join the family of the Church through the Sacrament of Baptism. In receiving this Sacrament we are 'plunged into' the person of Jesus Christ in mystery. We are not going to fully understand how this happens but St. Paul says we have 'put on' or are 'clothed in' Christ Jesus in a very personal way (Gal. 3:27). It is as if we are born again into the very life of God and are cleansed of original sin.

"The gathering of the People of God begins with Baptism; a church must have a place for the celebration of Baptism and for fostering remembrance of the baptismal promises (holy water font)." CCC 1185

We are all children of the family of God, because God loves us so much in his Son Jesus that God makes us one with Jesus, the child of God. So we all pray to the same Father.

You may need to explain that Catholics are Christians.

KEY QUESTIONS (To share with children at any point)

How do you think you become part of the family of the Church?

Have you ever seen a Baptism? What happened?

Introductory Activity

Draw something you like which belongs to you.

Tell the person beside you how you look after it.

Link Sentence

We all belong to God's family and God looks after us and we look after each other.

Now we are going to find out about our Church family.

Families and Celebrations

Look at the picture on page 18 in Big Book: **Baptism**

> We belong to a special family, the family of the Church.
> Lots of people belong to our Church family.
>
> When we are baptised we become members of the Church.

Questions to ask on picture in Big Book:

- What do you see in the picture?
- Who is there?
- What do you think is happening?

Text of story to read:

It was Sunday at last! Marcus and Joe were awake early and dressed in their best clothes.

Today, they were taking their baby sister to be baptised. The whole family would be there to see baby Anna become part of the Christian family. Marcus and Joe were very excited. They could not remember their own baptisms but they had seen the photographs in the album and Mummy had told them all about it.

The church was full of people who had come to Mass. "That's good," said Dad. "Lots of people to welcome our baby into the Church."

The front seat had been kept free for them. Father Peter came and said 'Hello' to them before Mass. At the last minute, Auntie Jill and Uncle David arrived. They were going to be the baby's Godparents.

When the time came, Father Peter welcomed the whole family and made the sign of the cross on Anna's forehead. He asked the family and the Godparents to come and stand around the baptismal font. He made sure that Marcus and Joe could see everything that was happening. Then Father Peter blessed Anna with holy oil. Marcus and Joe listened as Mummy and Daddy, Auntie Jill and Uncle David made baptismal promises for Anna. They would all help Anna to be a good child of God

Families and Celebrations

and grow up in the Christian family.

Then Father Peter poured the holy water over Anna's head three times and said the words of Baptism: "I baptise you in the name of the Father and of the Son and of the Holy Spirit." A white shawl was wrapped around Anna and she was given a Baptismal candle.

Afterwards, everyone was very happy. Back at home, they had a party with all the family and friends. One day, Marcus and Joe would tell Anna about the day she was baptised.

Questions to ask on story:

- What did the priest do when he baptised the baby?

- What did he say?

- Why do you think the family had a party?

Activities:

1. Ask pupils to bring a copy of a photograph of their own baptism to be put into a photo album entitled "Joining the Church Family." The photograph could include family members and friends at their Baptism. *(The class teacher perhaps could bring one).*

2. **Work Book** page 19 'Paul is Baptised'.

3. Have a display of Baptismal items, e.g. christening robe *(this can often be purchased at a second hand shop)* /water/oil/prayer book etc. all labelled. Children can write their own (full) names on a card to place on Baptismal table. *(The school usually has a register of full names).* Joining the Church Family Album can also be placed on this table.

4. Use a globe (that lights up, if possible). Children put their stand up figures around it saying 'We belong to God's Family, the biggest family in the world'. These words could be on a large poster behind the globe.

5. **Sing and act** out words of 'Sing for Joy' or 'Though we are many' from Share the Light'. Available from Viewpoint Direct Resources, Fax. 020 8692 0375

ICT for children: www.dottieandbuzz.co.uk click on 'Baptism' and you will find a variety of activities.

Following Jesus

1.4 Following Jesus

Catechism of the Catholic Church
"From the beginning, Jesus associated his disciples with his own life, revealed the mystery of the Kingdom to them and gave them a share in his mission, joy and sufferings." CCC 787

AT1 & AT2
Learning ABOUT and learning FROM the Catholic Faith

Key Learning Objectives
In this unit you will have the opportunity to:

- Hear how Jesus chose some of the first disciples (Lk. 3, 5:1-11).
  - Reflect on how we choose our friends.

- Know how Jesus taught his disciples to pray (Mt. 6: 7-15).
  - Reflect on how we pray.

- Hear the story of the Good Samaritan.
  - Reflect on the message it has for us as followers of Jesus.

- Hear the story of Jesus and his followers going into Jerusalem.
  - Think of how we can show that we 'welcome' Jesus.

- Know that Jesus died on Good Friday but that this is not the end of the story.
  - Reflect on the time of waiting before Easter Sunday.

Theological Notes

Q. What is most important about the call of the first disciples?
One day Jesus was preaching the Word of God on the shores of the Lake Galilee. The crowds were pressing in on him. He noticed two boats moored to the shore, the fishermen had left them to go and wash their nets. Getting into Simon Peter's boat, he asked him to move a little way into the water so that he could speak to the crowd. When he had finished speaking, Jesus said to Peter: "Launch out into the deep, and let down your nets for a catch". Peter reacted in all sincerity: "Master, we have toiled and laboured all night, and have caught nothing!" But he added immediately: "But, Master, at **your** Word I shall let down the nets." He did so, and there was such a huge catch of fish that the nets were at breaking-point – so much so, that Peter had to cry out for help from his companions in the other boat. Noticing that the two boats were filled with an immense haul of fish and were about to sink under its weight, Peter fell at the feet of Jesus and cried out: "Depart from

me, for I am a sinful man, O Lord!" Peter recognised in Jesus the Holy One of God, and openly acknowledged his own sinfulness before the holiness of this Master and Lord. This same Lord and Master, now lifted him up and said: "Do not be afraid, Peter; from now on, you will be catching not fish, but people". "And when they (Peter and his companions) had brought their boats to land, they left everything (boats, nets and all) and followed him" (Lk. 5:1-11).

Q. How did Jesus teach his disciples to pray?
Luke tells us that one of Jesus' disciples asked him to teach them how to pray, as John taught his disciples. (Lk 11:1) Jesus, here and in a longer version (Mt. 6) gives the disciples a beautiful pattern of prayer, called the 'Our Father' from its first words, or the Lord's Prayer, because it was given by the Lord. In telling his disciples to address God as 'Father', a term used within the family, Jesus quietly presents one of the foundational mysteries of Christianity. Not only is God 'Father' in the sense that He creates and sustains everything; He is also eternally Father because He has a Son who is 'eternally begotten', a Son who has always been with Him. In uniting himself to humanity in the Incarnation, Jesus now makes it possible for us, united to him in Baptism and the Sacraments, to call God 'Father'. We are invited to share in the very life of the Trinity itself. This is new - it is the Good News of the Gospel.

Q. What is the significance of Jesus going to Jerusalem?
When Jesus and his disciples entered Jerusalem, it was a clear proclamation of Jesus as king and God. Matthew points out that Jesus rode into Jerusalem to fulfil the prophecy of Zechariah 9:9 "Behold your king comes to you, meek and sitting upon an ass." People were shouting 'Hosanna' because they recognised Jesus as their king, but 'Hosanna' is an expression that is only addressed to God, and means 'Save us'! The authorities in Jerusalem were not happy that the people were hailing Jesus as king, especially when they shouted 'Hosanna'.

A few days later the authorities had raised a great crowd against Jesus, a mob who howled for his death. Jesus died publicly and shamefully on the cross, so all could see his death was a real death. He died in obedience to his Father, to whom he handed himself over in love. He died from love as he handed himself over to us, with words of forgiveness, and words of hope as he gave us his Mother to be ours. Because Jesus is joined with humanity in the Incarnation, and we now share his divine life through Baptism, we too can hope to pass through death as he did and live a new life with him. (See CCC 627).

Following Jesus

Jesus chooses the First Disciples

> Hear how Jesus chose some of the first disciples.
> Reflect on how we choose our friends.

Scripture text and notes for Teachers

The first four disciples are called

"Now Jesus was standing one day by the Lake of Gennesaret, with the crowd pressing round him listening to the word of God, when he caught sight of two boats close to the bank. The fishermen had gone out of them and were washing their nets. He got into one of the boats – it was Simon's – and asked him to put out a little from the shore. Then he sat down and taught the crowds from the boat.

When he had finished speaking he said to Simon, 'Put out into deep water and pay out your nets for a catch'. 'Master,' Simon replied 'we worked hard all night long and caught nothing, but if you say so, I will pay out the nets.' And when they had done this they caught such a huge number of fish that their nets began to tear, so they signalled to their companions in the other boat to come and help them; when these came, they filled the two boats to sinking point.

When Simon Peter saw this he fell at the knees of Jesus saying, 'Leave me, Lord; I am a sinful man'. For he and all his companions were completely overcome by the catch they had made; so also were James and John, sons of Zebedee, who were Simon's partners. But Jesus said to Simon, 'Do not be afraid; from now on it is men you will catch'. Then, bringing their boats back to land, they left everything and followed him." (Lk. 5:1-11)

Notes for Teacher

Help the children to understand that Jesus chose his friends, not for what they were or could do at that time – they were simple fishermen – but for what they would do and become, and for their trust in him. All the time Jesus was with these, his friends, he loved and accepted them – each and all – just as they were.

Explain that we call the friends of Jesus his disciples and that this means followers.

KEY QUESTIONS (To share with children at any point)

Why do you think Jesus chose some special friends?

What do you think Jesus liked most of all about Peter? *(That he did what he was told to do, i.e. put down his net into the water again.)*

Why do you think Peter and his friends left their boats behind and went with Jesus?

Following Jesus

Introductory Activity
Have two large cut-outs of children [a boy and a girl] with the words, "My friend" on them. Invite children to give their own reasons why someone might be chosen to be a friend, e.g. 'He makes me laugh'. Teacher could write them up.

Link Sentence
Now let us find out how Jesus chose his friends.

Look at the picture on page 19 in Big Book: Following Jesus
Questions on picture in Big Book

> Jesus said, "Peter, put your net down into the water and see what you will catch."
>
> Then Jesus said, "You will not be catching fish, you will bring people to me".

- Who can you see in the picture?

- What is happening?

- Why do you think they are now catching lots of fish?

- What do you think Jesus meant when he told Peter he will be bringing people to him?

Text to read to children:
Jesus had a lot of work to do. He wanted all the people in the world to know about God. So he needed some helpers.

Simon Peter and Andrew were fishermen. One day, when they were busy mending their fishing nets, a large crowd arrived. "What's going on?" Simon Peter shouted. "It's Jesus, everybody is talking about him", said Andrew.

Following Jesus

Just then Jesus arrived and got into Simon Peter's boat and asked them to pull away from the shore. Jesus spoke to the crowd from the boat. Then he said to Simon Peter and Andrew. "Take your boat further out to sea and put out your fishing nets". Simon said, "Master, we have worked hard all night and caught nothing, but if you say so, we will do it".

They could not believe it! The fish came rushing into their nets. They caught so many that they had to call James and John to come and help them in their boat.

They were all amazed at what had happened. They believed Jesus was someone very special. Then Jesus told them that he wanted them to stay with him, not to catch fish, but to bring people to him. So they left their fishing boats behind and went with Jesus.

Questions to ask:

- What do you think you would need to be a fisherman? What would you have to be good at? *[Be strong; staying awake at night, patience, able to handle boat • and mend nets, ability to get on with others, experience, work as part of a team, trust each other, not be afraid when storms came….]*

- Why didn't Simon Peter want to put the nets in the water again? *[Tired, thought it would be no good, didn't know Jesus…]*

- Why do you think he did put the nets in the water again after all? *[Something made him trust Jesus. Something about Jesus, but also something from within himself.]*

- How do you think Peter, James and John felt when they decided to leave their fishing boats behind and follow Jesus? *[Excited, frightened, what would people think? Would they have enough money to buy food?*

Activities
1. a) Draw a picture of your friend. Write his or her name by the picture.

   b) Choose one or two of the sentences (on the board) to show why you chose that person to be your friend and copy them by the picture. You might want to write another sentence of your own.
   (Teacher will need to display sentences where children can see them and provide a prompt for the less able e.g. … is my friend because …)

2. **Work Book** page 20 'Jesus & the Fishermen'.

3. Power Point Presentation 'Jesus and the Fishermen' available from the Teachers' Enterprise in Religious Education, email for details: info@tere.org

5. **Listen** to story 'Jesus and Peter go fishing' CD Stories & Songs of Jesus, available from McCrimmons Publishing, 10-12 High Street, Great Wakering, Essex SS3 0EQ FAX 01702 216082; also St. Pauls; Pauline Multi Media.

6. Children put actions to the **song**: 'Fishing for People' CD Stories & Songs of Jesus.

Jesus teaches the disciples to pray

Know that Jesus taught his disciples to pray.
Reflect on how we pray.

Scripture text for Teachers

The Lord's prayer
"Now once Jesus was in a certain place praying, and when he had finished one of his disciples said, 'Lord, teach us to pray, just as John taught his disciples'. He said to them, 'Say this when you pray:
Father, may your name be held holy,
your kingdom come;
give us each day our daily bread,
and forgive us our sins,
for we ourselves forgive each one who is in debt to us.
And do not put us to the test.'" (Lk. 11:1-4)

Note: Small children often mishear the unfamiliar words, so it can be helpful for them to see it written out.

KEY QUESTIONS (To share with children at any point)
Why do you think Jesus' disciples asked him to teach them how to pray?
Why do you think Jesus told them to call God 'Our Father'?

Following Jesus

Introductory Activity
Ask the children if they ever talk to God. Explain that we call this prayer.
Invite children to tell you any prayers that they say, formal or informal. Ask if the children know the Our Father - perhaps they will have said it at home, at church, or in the classroom or assembly.
Have a large print version available to display. (See page 89).

Link Sentence
Now we are going to hear about how Jesus taught his friends to pray.

Look at the picture on page 20 in the Big Book: Jesus and the Disciples

One day, Jesus' friends asked him to teach them how to pray.

Jesus taught them to pray to 'Our Father in heaven'.

His friends were happy. They knew God was their Father too.

Questions on picture in Big Book

- Who do you see in the picture?

- What do you think Jesus is doing?

- Why do you think he is kneeling down?

- When do we kneel down? Why?

- What do you think Jesus' friends are saying to him?

Text to read to children
One day, Jesus was praying to God his Father. Jesus prayed every day because he loved his Father and wanted to stay close to Him.

Following Jesus

Jesus' friends had noticed that he prayed. They watched him, and they wanted to pray to God the Father in the same way. But they didn't know how.

One of Jesus' friends decided to ask Jesus what to do. He waited until Jesus had finished praying and he went up to him.

"Jesus," he said quietly, "Will you teach us how to pray?"

Jesus smiled at his friends and gathered them round him.

"You can pray like this," he said, and he began to tell them how they could talk to God and call him their Father in heaven. He told them that they could ask God for anything they needed and say 'sorry' for wrong things they had done.

Questions to ask on story:

- Why do you think Jesus prayed to God his Father?
  [*To ask for help, to be close to him, because he had a difficult job to do, because he was concerned for people, just because he loved his Father.*]

- What do you think Jesus' friends thought when they saw him praying?
  [*They wished he would stop and talk to them, they wished they knew how to pray, they wondered what he was saying.*]

- What do you think you need to be able to pray?
  [*A quiet place, someone to help you and tell you what to do, some people to pray with, to be on your own, to be in church, you just need to want to pray, you need Jesus to help you.*]

- What do you think the disciples thought when Jesus told them they could call God 'Father' too?
  [*They had a new family, they were close to God, they were like brothers to Jesus, they were God's children in a special way now.*]

Activities

1. Display a large print version of the Our Father and invite children to pray it with you. (See page 89)

   Ask children to come up and highlight, ring round, underline or tell you any words they don't understand.

   Have the most likely words on cards which can be displayed nearby for future reference.

   Activity continued on next page

Following Jesus

Explain a few meanings, depending on the children's ability and level of concentration. These can be revised or continued periodically. Simple definitions could be displayed also.

2. Teach the children a sung version, perhaps with actions. The 'Echo' Our Father is useful for helping children learn the words.

3. Make a class or group book for display called, "How to Pray". Help children to offer suggestions based on the Our Father, such as: Remember you are one of God's children; Remember God's name is holy; Ask God for what you need; Say sorry if you have done something wrong; Forgive people who hurt you; Ask God to help you stay out of trouble.

4. **Listen** to the story of: 'Jesus teaches the disciples to pray' and song 'The Lord's Prayer' on CD 'More Stories & Songs of Jesus' by Paule Freeburg, DC & Christopher Walker. Available from McCrimmons Publishing; St. Pauls or Pauline Multi Media.

The Good Samaritan

Hear the story of the Good Samaritan.
Reflect on the message it has for us as followers of Jesus.

Scripture text for Teachers

Parable of the Good Samaritan
"A man was once on his way down from Jerusalem to Jericho and fell into the hands of brigands; they took all he had, beat him and then made off, leaving him half dead. Now a priest happened to be travelling down the same road, but when he saw the man, he passed by on the other side. In the same way a Levite who came to the place saw him, he passed by on the other side. But a Samaritan traveller who came upon him was moved with compassion when he saw him. He went up and bandaged his wounds, pouring oil and wine on them. He then lifted him on to his own mount, carried him to the inn and looked after him. Next day, he took out two denarii and handed them to the innkeeper, 'Look after him,' he said 'and on my way back I will make good any extra expense you have.' Which of these three, do you think, proved himself a neighbour to the man who fell into the brigands' hands?' 'The one who took pity on him,' he replied. Jesus said to him, 'Go, and do the same yourself'. (Lk. 10:29-37)

Note: Emphasise that Jesus asks each one of us to be kind and thoughtful when we see anyone in difficulty and do what we can to help them.

Following Jesus

KEY QUESTIONS (To share with children at any point)
Why do you think Jesus told stories?
Why do you think Jesus told the story of the Good Samaritan?

Introductory Activity
Teacher accidentally drops a box of objects, leaves them on the floor and waits to see which children will come forward to help. Then the teacher makes a special point of thanking them for their kindness.
Remind children of how they have shown kindness in the past.

Link Sentence
Now we are going to hear about somebody else who needed help.

Look at the picture on page 21 in Big Book: The Good Samaritan

A man was going on a long journey.

He was attacked by robbers.
A stranger helped the man.

He was a good neighbour.

Questions on picture in Big Book

- Who do you see in the picture?

- What do you think is going to happen to the man?

- What else do you see?

Text to read to children
One day Jesus told this story.
A traveller was going on a long journey. It was a dangerous journey because often there were robbers looking for people to attack. The traveller walked along hoping he

Following Jesus

would be all right. Then suddenly, a group of men jumped out from behind the trees and beat him up. They took everything he had and left him lying on the road badly injured.

The traveller hoped someone would come past to help. Soon he saw a priest, but the priest walked on pretending not to see him. Then another important person came along. But he walked over to the other side of the road and did not even look at him. After a while, a man from another country came along. He was a Samaritan and the traveller thought he was an enemy. But what a surprise! The Samaritan stopped and said: 'You are badly hurt. Let me help you'. He put a bandage on his wounds, put him on his donkey and took him to an inn. He gave the people at the inn money to look after him until he was better and he said he would pay for anything else when he came back.

Then Jesus asked the crowd: 'Which of the three people who saw the injured man was a good neighbour to him'. They replied, 'The man who helped him'. Then Jesus said that we must do the same.

Questions on picture and story:

- How do you think the man felt as he walked along the road?

- Suddenly, something happened – what was it?

- Why do you think the priest and the important person did not stop to help?

- How do you think the injured man felt when he saw a stranger coming over to him?

- What did he do for him?

- What did he say to the people at the inn?

- Why do you think Jesus told us this story?

- What does he want us to remember about it?

- How can we be 'Good Samaritans' to others at home and at school?

Activities
1. **Work Book** page 21 'The Good Samaritan'.

2. Role-play story of the Good Samaritan.
   You will need: man on a journey, robbers, priest, important person, Samaritan and people at the inn.

Following Jesus

3. **Listen** to story 'The Good Man from Samaria' CD Stories & Songs of Jesus, available from McCrimmons Publishing, 10-12 High Street, Great Wakering, Essex SS3 0EQ FAX 01702 216082; also St. Pauls; Pauline Multi Media.

4. Learn **song** 'I'll help you' CD Stories & Songs of Jesus. The song is about the Good Samaritan.

5. Power Point Presentation 'The Good Samaritan' available from Teachers' Enterprise in Religious Education, email info@tere.org for details.

6. **ICT for children** www.reonline.co.uk click 'Bible' for story of Good Samaritan. www.request.org.uk Select 'Infants' then 'the Life of Jesus' then 'Tell me a story' then 'The Good Samaritan.

Jesus goes to Jerusalem

Hear the story of Jesus and his followers going to Jerusalem.
Think of how we can show that we 'welcome' Jesus.

Scripture text and notes for Teachers

The Messiah enters Jerusalem
"When Jesus was near Bethphage and Bethany, close by the Mount of Olives as it is called, he sent two of the disciples, telling them, 'Go to the village opposite, and as you enter it you will find a tethered colt that no one has yet ridden. Untie it and bring it here. If anyone asks you, 'Why are you untying it?' you are to say this, 'the Master needs it'. The messengers went off and found everything just as he had told them. As they were untying the colt, its owner said, 'Why are you untying that colt?' and they answered, 'The Master needs it'.

So they took the colt to Jesus, and throwing their garments over its back they helped Jesus on to it. As he moved off, people spread their cloaks in the road, and now, as he was approaching the downward slope of the Mount of Olives, the whole group of disciples joyfully began to praise God at the top of their voices for all the miracles they had seen. They cried out:
'Blessings on the King who comes, in the name of the Lord!
Peace in heaven and glory in the highest heavens!'" (Lk. 19:28-38)

Continued on next page...

Following Jesus

Notes:
Explain to children that Jesus was coming to the most important place in his country, that he was coming there as king, though not the kind of king people were expecting and that most people were happy to see him.

The cloaks worn were just a large piece of material that people wrapped round them to keep them warm – like a coat without sleeves – but it was probably the most precious item of clothing that most people had. Spreading cloaks and palm branches was a way of honouring someone important as it kept the dust down and stopped them getting so dirty on the unmade roads.

We celebrate this event on Passion Sunday in church; a week before Easter Sunday.

KEY QUESTIONS (To share with children at any point)
Why do you think Jesus was going to Jerusalem?
Why do you think all the people were excited?

Introductory Activity
What do you think we could do to welcome a very important person to our school?

Link sentence
We are now going to hear about a big welcome Jesus received.

Look at the picture on page 22 in Big Book:
Jesus goes to Jerusalem

Jesus and his friends are coming to Jerusalem.

Jesus is riding on a donkey.
The people are happy to see him.

They shout 'Hosanna'.

Following Jesus

Questions to ask on picture in Big Book
- Who do you see in the picture?

- What is Jesus doing?

- What are the people doing?

- What do you think they are saying?

- How many people do you think are there?

- Why do you think there are so many people?

- Is everyone happy? Why?

Text to read to children

Jesus knew it was time for him to go to Jerusalem. Jerusalem was a very important city. The house of God was there. It was called the Temple. The Temple was a very special place where people were taught about God.

Jesus called two of his disciples to him. "Go into the next village," he told them, "and you will find a young donkey tied up outside one of the houses. No-one has ever ridden on it before. I want you to untie it and bring it to me. If anyone asks you what you are doing with the donkey, just say, 'The Lord needs it, but he will send it back afterwards.'"

So the two disciples went into the village. They found the donkey tied up by a doorway. They untied it and started to lead it away. The people who owned the donkey rushed out: "Why are you untying that donkey?" they asked.
"The Lord needs it," the disciples answered, "but he will send it back to you again."

So the people let them go and they took the donkey to Jesus. They spread their cloaks over its back and Jesus sat on the donkey's back. The donkey began to walk along the road to Jerusalem and lots more people came to walk with them. They spread their cloaks in the road and cut down branches from the trees and spread them in the road too, so that the donkey could walk over them. Everyone shouted, "Hosanna, hosanna!" The people in the city wondered who was coming when they heard all the noise! (Luke 19: 28-38)

Questions on picture and story:
- Why was Jesus going to Jerusalem?

- What was the name of the place he was going to visit? *(the Temple)*

- How did he manage to make this long journey – did he have a car?

Following Jesus

- Did the friends of Jesus have to buy the donkey? What did they do to get it?

- Why do you think a cloak was put on the donkey's back? *[To honour Jesus, donkey might have had dusty, itchy back, wanted to do something kind.]*

- How did the people show their welcome for Jesus? What did they do?

- Why do you think the people were giving him a big welcome?

- Do you think everyone would have been happy to see Jesus? Why? Why not?

- What would you have done if you had been there?

Activities:

1. **Work Book** page 22 'Jesus goes to Jerusalem'.

2. Make a 'Welcome Jesus' display as a class. Put a picture of Jesus in the centre, photographs or paintings of the children as the crowd – if they want to be part of the display. 'Welcome' could be written in many different fonts and colours and languages (if other languages are spoken at home).

3. Imagine you are a reporter and you are going to interview people in the crowd who are with Jesus. This could be:
   - hotseating
   - written task
   - role-play

4. **Listen** to story 'Hosanna to the Lord' CD More Stories and Songs of Jesus, available from McCrimmons Publishing, 10-12 High Street, Great Wakering, Essex SS3 0EQ FAX 01702 216082; also St. Pauls; Pauline Multi Media.

5. Learn **song** 'Sing Hosanna' CD More Stories and Songs of Jesus.
   "Sing hosanna, sing hosanna to the King.
   The children came with olive branches ...."

ICT for children: www.request.org.uk Select 'Festivals' then 'Easter' then 'Jesus comes to Jerusalem (Palm Sunday).

Following Jesus

Good Friday

> Know that Jesus died on Good Friday but that is not the end of the story.
> Think about when sad news turns into good news.

Scripture text and notes for Teachers

The relevant scripture texts are in Mark chapters 14, 15 and John 20. The following are extracts.

Conspiracy against Jesus:
"It was two days before the Passover and the feast of Unleavened Bread, and the chief priests and the scribes were looking for a way to arrest Jesus by some trick and have him put to death." (Mk. 14:1)

After the Last Supper Jesus goes to Gethsemane with the disciples:
"They came to a small estate celled Gethsemane, and Jesus said to his disciples, 'Stay here while I pray'. Then he took Peter and James and John with him. And a sudden fear came over him, and great distress. And he said to them, 'My soul is sorrowful to the point of death. Wait here, and keep awake.' And going on a little further he threw himself on the ground and prayed that, if it were possible, this hour might pass him by. 'Abba (Father)!' he said 'Everything is possible for you. Take this cup away from me. But let it be as you, not I, would have it.' He came back and found them sleeping and he said to Peter, 'Simon are you asleep? Had you not the strength to keep awake one hour?' ... 'Get up, let us go! My betrayer is close at hand already.'"

Jesus is arrested (Mk. 14:43-52).
Jesus is brought before the Sanhedrin (Mk. 14:53-65).
When Peter was asked if he was with Jesus he denied it (14:66-72).
Jesus brought before Pilate (Mk. 15:1-15).
Jesus crowned with thorns (15:16-20).

The crucifixion:
"It was the third hour when they crucified him. The inscription giving the charge against him read: 'The King of the Jews' (Mk. 5:26).

The burial (Mk. 15:42-47).
The empty tomb and the appearance of the risen Jesus (Jn. 20).

Notes: The aim is to help children to grasp that Jesus' death and resurrection are together one single mystery of handing over himself in love to God and to us.

One day, we will die but we believe that we too will rise from the dead and be in heaven with Jesus.

Following Jesus

KEY QUESTIONS (To share with children at any point)
What do we remember on Good Friday?
What do you think is going to happen next?

Introductory Activity
Have a 'Good Friday' bag containing relevant objects. (Cross, crucifix, large stone, hot cross bun, some flowers, model of Roman soldier.) Hold up objects one by one and ask children how they think these remind us of Good Friday when Jesus died?

Link sentence:
Today we are going to find out more about Good Friday.

Look at picture on page 23 in Big Book: Good Friday

> Jesus died on the cross on Good Friday, but...
> this is not the end of the story.
>
> His friends were very sad, but they waited patiently.
>
> Three days later, something wonderful happened!

Questions to ask on picture in Big Book
- Who can you see in the picture?

- How do you think they feel?

Text to read to children
When Jesus came to Jerusalem he went to the Temple. The Temple was God's house and Jesus sat there and taught people about God. He did this because he wanted them to know more about God and to be closer to Him. Not everyone was pleased about this. Some important people in the Temple were jealous of Jesus. They were jealous because they did not want Jesus to be more important than them. So they made a plan to have him killed. They even got one of Jesus' best friends to help them.

Following Jesus

One dark night, when the crowds had gone home and Jesus was praying in a quiet garden, his enemies came to arrest him. They took him away and treated him cruelly all night. When the next day came, Jesus was taken to a place outside Jerusalem and there he was left to die on a wooden cross. He was almost alone. Even his friends had run away. Only his mother Mary, and one friend, John, stayed with him.

At the end of the day, one of Jesus' friends found a special place for his body to lie. It was in a garden. The Roman soldiers came and rolled a huge rock in front of the place where Jesus' body lay. All Jesus' enemies laughed. He's gone forever now, they thought. Some of the women and the disciples crept back to watch. They saw where Jesus was lying, and they saw the huge stone. I wonder what they were thinking? [*Pause for children to offer ideas.*]

Every year we remember this day. We call it Good Friday, even though it didn't seem very good to Jesus' friends that day. But they didn't know the end of the story.... They had to wait for three days, and those days must have seemed very, very long.

Questions to ask on picture and story:

- Who can tell me what happened on Good Friday?

- Can anyone remember anything else?

- Does anyone know why some people wanted to have Jesus killed?

- Who stayed with Jesus when he was dying?

- What do you think Mary and the disciples did after Jesus had been laid in the garden and the heavy rock rolled in front?

Text to read to children: A big surprise

Very early in the morning, on the first day of the week, some women were tiptoeing through the early sunshine. Three days ago Jesus had died, so they felt very sad. They were going to see the garden where he had been buried.

What a surprise they had when they arrived! There were angels in the garden and the angels had the most amazing news.

"Jesus is risen from the dead!" said the angels, and the women were so surprised that they ran back and fetched some of Jesus' special friends.

Questions to ask on story:
- What do you think the women told the disciples, Jesus' special friends?

- Do you think they believed them? Why?

Following Jesus

Activities

1. a) Teacher makes 'zigzag books'. (Fold sheet of paper in half and fold again.)
   b) Teacher discusses with the children the events the story identifying the following key points which children will write/draw in their 'zigzag' books
   - Jesus rides on a donkey
   - Jesus is put on a cross
   - Most of the disciples run away
   - Jesus is laid in the garden with a big rock in front.
   - The women are watching to see where he is laid.
   - This story helps me to remember .....

   c) Choose one important 'frame' to talk about – the one you like best.

2. a) On Good Friday, Jesus' friends were sad. Draw a sad face.
   b) On Easter Sunday, Jesus' friends were happy. Draw a happy face.
   c) Write what changed sad faces into happy faces.

3. Learn appropriate, joyful Easter song, hymn or chorus. Use percussion instruments to accompany it.

4. Reflective activity for teacher to lead.
   If appropriate, talk about the hope that Easter gives. Death was not the end for Jesus. He says it will not be the end for us either. Explain that death is like the blowing out of a candle that is then relit. Use a self-lighting candle or light a candle and blow it out and relight it.

ICT for children: www.request.org.uk Select 'Infants' then 'Festivals' then 'Easter' then 'Jesus dies on a cross (Good Friday)

The Lord's Prayer

Our Father, who art in heaven,
hallowed be thy name;
thy Kingdom come;
thy will be done on earth as it is in heaven.

Give us this day our daily bread;
and forgive us our trespasses as we forgive those who trespass against us.

And lead us not into temptation but deliver us from evil. Amen.

The Resurrection

1.5 The Resurrection

Catechism of the Catholic Church
"Jesus Christ's Resurrection – and the risen Christ himself – is the principle and source of *our future resurrection*: 'Christ has been raised from the dead, the first fruits of those who have fallen asleep... For as in Adam all die, so also in Christ shall all be made alive.'"
CCC 655.

AT1 & AT2
Learning ABOUT and learning FROM the Catholic Faith

Key Learning Objectives
In this unit you will have the opportunity to:

- Know that we celebrate the resurrection of Jesus at Easter.
  - Reflect on how we do this.

- Know that Jesus rose from the dead on the first Easter Sunday.
  - Reflect on what this means for us.

- Know that Jesus appeared to the disciples in the Upper Room.
  - Think about the times when we have experienced big surprises.

- Know that Jesus helped the disciples to understand that he was truly alive.
  - Think about how happy everybody was to see him.

- Know that Thomas did not believe that Jesus was alive.
  - Reflect on times when we don't understand what is happening.

- Know that Jesus returned to heaven after forty days.
  - Reflect on the promises he made.

Theological Notes

Q. What does it mean to say that Jesus is risen from the dead?
"Christ's Resurrection was not a return to earthly life, as was the case with the raisings from the dead that he had performed before Easter: Jairus' daughter, the young man of Nain, Lazarus. These actions were miraculous events, but the persons miraculously raised returned by Jesus' power to ordinary earthly life. At some particular moment they would die again. Christ's Resurrection is essentially different. In his risen body he passes from the state of death to another life beyond time and space." (CCC646)

The Resurrection

Q. What does the Resurrection mean for us?
The Risen Jesus gives us in all these promises the assurance, that the Spirit that he and his Father will send, is the Spirit of Truth, the Comforter, the Advocate. Now the Risen Jesus actually fulfilled this promise, the promise we have had in the Last Supper discourse in the Gospel of St. John, chapters 14, 15 and 16. The actual gift of the Spirit was brought by the Risen Jesus when he appeared to his disciples who, for fear of the Jews, had locked themselves behind closed doors. They were all huddled together under one roof, yet there was among them no community. It is not because persons are huddled together under one roof that there is necessarily community. The disciples had lost faith in Jesus – the key to, and secret of, Christian community. They thought everything was over; their world and worldly hopes were shattered by the death of Jesus on the cross. Afraid of the Jews, they locked themselves behind closed doors. And Jesus – the Risen Jesus – broke through these closed doors and closed hearts – and said: "Peace be with you". Then he added: "Receive the Holy Spirit". He had earlier promised them the Spirit. Now he gave them that Spirit, the Spirit of peace and reconciliation. For the Risen Jesus continued: "Whose sins you will forgive, they are forgiven them, whose sins you retain, they are retained" (cf. Jn. 20:21-23). The Spirit of Peace and Reconciliation!

Easter

> **Know that we celebrate the Resurrection of Jesus at Easter.**
> **Reflect on how we do this.**

KEY QUESTIONS (To share with children at any point)
Why do you think we celebrate at Easter?
What do you think the 'resurrection' means?

Look at page 24 in Big Book:
The Resurrection

At Easter, we celebrate with other people.

We are happy that Jesus rose from the dead.

We know that we will be able to be with him one day.

91

The Resurrection

Questions on picture in Big Book
- What do you think this picture is about?

- Where is the family preparing to go? Why?

- What do you see on the table? Why?

Text to read to children:
It is Easter Sunday morning, cold and bright in the spring sunshine. Just a little while ago, David and Jenny were still fast asleep in bed. Now they are up and dressed in their best clothes.

"Come on!" says Granny. "We don't want to be late for Mass on the most important day of the year!"

As they hurry off down the road, Jenny asks her Dad why Easter is the most important day in the year. "I thought the most important day was Christmas!" said David.

Dad laughed. "Easter is the most important because Jesus rose from the dead on that day," he told them. "Jesus is the Son of God. When he died on the cross, he went right through death and came out on the other side! He made a way for us to do that too, when the time comes. That's why Easter is so important. We are happy because Jesus is alive again. And we are happy because he has made a way for us to be with him one day."

Questions to ask about the story:
- Can you remember which day Jenny's dad said was the most important?

- Why did he say that Easter was the most important?

- What can you do at Easter to show Jesus that you want to thank him for all he did for us?

Activities
1. Make an Easter Cross. Explain to the children that they will decorate an empty cross to celebrate Jesus rising from the dead using something that everyone thought was finished with.
   Teachers may wish to use the following idea: Cut out, or help a child to cut two identical waxed paper crosses. Supply children with shreds of coloured wax crayons that were so old and broken that they were useless. [An adult may need to shave or grate the crayons]. Sprinkle crayons onto one waxed paper cross in a pattern, then cover with the second paper cross. An adult irons the paper. The crosses can be hung in the window to catch the sunshine.

The Resurrection

> 2. Prepare an Easter celebration in the classroom. Children could bring flowers or make them. Tell children they are going to celebrate the gift of life that Jesus gives.
>
> 3. **ICT for children:** www.request.org.uk Select 'Infants' then 'Festivals' then 'Easter' then 'When is Easter Day?' and 'How do Christians celebrate Easter'.

Jesus rose from the dead

> Know that Jesus rose from the dead on the first Easter Sunday.
> Reflect on what this means for us.

Scripture text for Teachers

The empty tomb (Gospel of Mark)
"When the Sabbath was over, Mary of Magdala, Mary the mother of James, and Salome, brought spices with which to go and anoint Jesus. And very early in the morning on the first day of the week they went to the tomb, just as the sun was rising.

They had been saying to one another, 'Who will roll away the stone for us from the entrance to the tomb?' But when they looked they could see that the stone – which was very big – had already been rolled ack. On entering the tomb they saw a young man in a white robe seated on the right-hand side, and they were struck with amazement. But he said to them, 'There is no need for alarm. You are looking for Jesus of Nazareth, who was crucified: he has risen, he is not here. See, here is the place where they laid him. But you must go and tell his disciples and Peter, that he is going before you to Galilee; it is there you will see him, just as he told you'. And the women came out and ran away from the tomb because they were frightened out of their wits; and they said nothing to a soul, for they were afraid." (Mk. 16:1-8)

The appearance to Mary of Magdala (Gospel of John)
Meanwhile, Mary stayed outside near the tomb, weeping. Then, still weeping, she stooped to look inside, and saw two angels in white sitting where the body of Jesus had been, one at the head, the other at the feet. They said, 'Woman, why are you weeping?' 'They have taken my Lord away' she replied 'and I don't know where they have put him.' As she said this she turned round and saw Jesus standing there, though she did not recognise him. Jesus said, 'Woman, why are you weeping? Who are you looking for?' Supposing him to be the gardener, she said, 'Sir, if you have taken him away, tell me where you have put him, and I will go and remove him'. Jesus said, 'Mary!' She knew him then and said to him in Hebrew, 'Rabbuni!' which means Master. Jesus said to her, 'Do not cling to me, because I have not yet ascended to the Father and your Father, to my God and your God.' So Mary of Magdala went and told the disciples that she had seen the Lord and that he had said these things to her." (Jn. 20:11-18)

The Resurrection

KEY QUESTIONS (To share with children at any point)
What do you think the friends of Jesus thought when he died? How do you think the women felt when they saw angels in the garden?

Introductory Activity
Ask the children what they remember about the first Good Friday. (Perhaps show them a crucifix to remind them, or point to the one in the classroom.) If there is an Easter Garden in the classroom, indicate the empty tomb and the stone rolled back.

Link Sentence
Today, we are going to hear about the wonderful surprise some friends of Jesus had on the first Easter Day.

Look at the picture on page 25 in Big Book: Jesus appears to Mary of Magdala

> Jesus' friends felt sad because he had died.
>
> But now, he is alive and one of them has seen him!
> The others are running to see if it is true.

Questions on picture in Big Book

- What can you see in the picture? *(Can the children spot the tomb and the stone rolled away and Jesus talking to a woman, Mary of Magdala).*

- What do you think has happened?

- What do you think Jesus and his friend, Mary were saying to each other?
  (Explain that this Mary is not the Mother of Jesus, but one of his friends, also called Mary.)

- Why do you think Peter and John are running so fast?

- How do you think they feel?

The Resurrection

Text to read to children

Very early in the morning, on the first day of the week, some women were tiptoeing through the early sunshine. Three days ago Jesus had died, so they felt very sad. They were going to see the garden where he had been buried.

What a surprise they had when they arrived! There were angels in the garden and the angels had the most amazing news.

"Jesus is risen from the dead!" said the angels, and the women were so surprised that they ran back and fetched some of Jesus' special friends.

His friends ran to see where Jesus had been buried, but he wasn't there. There was just an empty tomb! They went slowly back home, thinking hard.

Mary of Magdala stayed in the garden. She couldn't believe it. She looked in the tomb again and started to cry.

Suddenly, she realised there was someone behind her. She turned round and saw a man standing there - she thought it was the gardener.

"Why are you crying?" the man asked her. Mary started to tell him that she didn't know where Jesus was. She felt very confused. But then the man spoke her name.

"Mary!" he said gently. At once Mary recognised Jesus - he really was alive! She felt so happy.

Jesus wasn't dead any more. The women saw him, and his friends saw him too, in the garden and in lots of other places.

What wonderful news. The women and the friends of Jesus told everyone about it, and that's how we know. Jesus is alive again. Alleluia!

Questions to ask about the story:

- Why were the women going to the garden?
  [*To see where Jesus had been buried; to be near Jesus even though they thought he was dead.*]

- What do you think the women were thinking about as they crept through the early morning sunshine?

- Does anyone know what day of the week it was when the women went to the garden? [*First day of the week, Sunday, Easter Sunday.*]

The Resurrection

- Who told the women that Jesus was alive?

- What did the women do when they heard the news?

- What do you think the friends of Jesus thought when the women came to fetch them and told them Jesus is alive again? *[Hope, fear, disbelief, ridicule, but they came anyway.]*

- What do you think 'Alleluia' might mean? *[Let children guess from context, but ensure they end up knowing it means 'praise God'.]*

Activities

1. a) Make a class 'Easter Garden'.
   Suggestions: include some small plants; a little box for the empty tomb and piece of white cloth in it. *(You may wish to take a photo of it to project onto the whiteboard so that all the children can see it).*
   b) Imagine you are in the garden.
   - What would you be thinking?
   - What would you see?
   - Who might you meet?
   - What would you say to them?

2. a) Children make a tableau of the women speaking to the disciples.
   b) The teacher suggests questions:
   - What are the women saying to the disciples?
   - What are the disciples saying?
   - Children bring their tableau to life and role-play the scene.

3. Listen to the story: 'Jesus is Alive', CD More Stories and Songs of Jesus.

4. Put actions to the song: 'I am here with you', CD More Stories and Songs of Jesus. Available from McCrimmons Publishing, 10-12 High Street, Great Wakering, Essex SS3 0EQ FAX 01702 216082; also St. Pauls; Pauline Multi Media.

The Resurrection

Jesus appears to the Disciples

> Know that Jesus appeared to the disciples in the Upper Room.
> Think about times when we have experienced big surprises.

Scripture text and notes for Teachers

Appearances to the disciples
"In the evening of that same day, the first day of the week, the doors were closed in the room where the disciples were, for fear of the Jews. Jesus came and stood among them. He said to them, 'Peace be with you', and showed them his hands and his side. The disciples were filled with joy when they saw the Lord, and he said to them again, 'Peace be with you'" (Jn. 20: 19-21)

Notes: Make sure children understand that 'disciples' refers here to the special friends of Jesus. They were taking refuge in the Upper Room because they were afraid and thought they might be captured as well.

KEY QUESTIONS (To share with children at any point)
What do you think the disciples did after Jesus died?
Do you think that they believed they would see him again?

Introductory Activity
Ask children:
What is the best surprise you have ever had?
Why was it such a surprise?
How did you feel?

Link Sentence
Today, we are going to hear about how the friends of Jesus had the most wonderful surprise ever!

The Resurrection

**Look at picture on page 26 in Big Book:
Jesus appears to the disciples.**

> The disciples were very worried after Jesus died.
> They thought they were on their own now.
> Suddenly Jesus was in the room with them!
>
> Jesus was alive! He said, "Peace be with you!"

Questions to ask on picture in Big Book
- Who can you see in the picture?
- Look at the disciples faces. How do you think they are feeling?
- How many disciples are there? Who is with them?

Text to read to children:

Have you ever felt a bit frightened and worried? [*Pause to allow children to respond.*] Well, Jesus' special friends, the disciples, felt like that after he died. They really didn't know what to do next. Should they go home and start working at their old jobs again? Should they stay in Jerusalem and wait for a good idea? They were afraid they would be caught and punished for being friends of Jesus. So they were hiding in an upstairs room, being very quiet and wondering what to do next. They were so frightened that they had even locked the door.

Suddenly, without the door even opening, Jesus was there in the room with them, holding out his arms to them and saying "Peace be with you!" The disciples were amazed, and even more scared than they had been before. They thought Jesus was dead! What do you think went through their minds when they saw him standing there? [*Pause to allow children to respond.*]

Questions to ask about picture and story:

- Why do you think the disciples were hiding in a locked room? [*Fear they would be treated the same way as Jesus, not sure what to do next.*]

The Resurrection

- When you look at the picture, what can you tell about the way the disciples were feeling when Jesus was suddenly in the room with them? [*Encourage children to look at individual faces and observe range of emotions.*]

- What did Jesus say to the disciples? [*Peace be with you!*]

- Why do you think he said, 'Peace be with you' before he said anything else to them? [*To reassure them, make them less scared, so they could recognise his voice which they would have known well.*]

Activities

1. Make a surprise picture with a 'lift-the-flap'. Picture can be of any happy occasion, perhaps one discussed in the introductory activity, but the surprise under the flap must be a happy one. Encourage children to show the expressions on the faces of those receiving the surprise.

2. **Work Book** page 23 'Jesus appears to the Disciples'.

3. Pretend you are Peter. Describe what happened in the Upper Room.

4. **ICT for children:** www.request.org.uk Select 'Infants' then 'Festivals' then 'Easter' then 'Jesus is alive' (Easter Sunday). Listen to the account of the Resurrection. Print the story and share it with your family.

5. **Listen** to story 'Jesus Lives' CD Stories and Songs of Jesus.

6. Learn **song** 'Jesus Lives' CD Stories and Songs of Jesus.

The Resurrection

Jesus eats with the Disciples

> Know that Jesus helped the disciples to understand that he was alive.
> Think about how happy everybody was to see him.

Scripture text and notes for Teachers

Jesus eats with the disciples
The disciples were still talking about all that had happened when Jesus himself stood among them and said to them, 'Peace be with you!' In a state of alarm and fright, they thought they were seeing a ghost. But he said, 'Why are you so agitated, and why are these doubts rising in your hearts? Look at my hands and feet; yes, it is I indeed. Touch me and see for yourselves; a ghost has no flesh and bones as you can see I have.' And as he said this he showed them his hands and feet. Their joy was so great that they still could not believe, and they stood there dumbfounded, so he said to them, 'Have you anything to eat?' And they offered him a piece of grilled fish, which he took and ate before their eyes". (Lk. 24:36-43)

Notes: Jesus appeared to his disciples to give them 'peace' and 'hope'; we recall they were 'afraid' and 'losing hope'. The disciples naturally supposed they were seeing a ghost as (a) the door was locked and (b) they had seen him die and be buried. Jesus encouraged them to touch him and he ate something. However, there must have been something different about him; for instance, he could pass through locked doors.

KEY QUESTIONS (To share with children at any point)
Why do you think Jesus appeared to the disciples?
How do you think they felt when they saw him?

Introductory Activity
Discuss: What does it feel like when you meet someone in a place where you did not expect to see them?
- Did you recognise them right away?
- What helped you to recognise them?
- Why do you think you did not recognise them straight away?

Link Sentence
Today, we are going to hear how Jesus helped his friends to recognise him and how astonished and excited they were to see him.

The Resurrection

**Look at picture on page 24 in Work Book:
Jesus eats with the disciples**

Jesus loved his friends.

He did not want them to be scared.

He ate some food to show them he was really alive.

Explain that the door was locked and yet Jesus appeared. They thought they were seeing a ghost. But Jesus loved his friends very much; he did not want them to be scared, so he ate some food to show them he really was alive!

Text to read to children:
Jesus looked round the room at his friends. He understood just how frightened they were. They had been scared even before he appeared and now they thought they were seeing a ghost! Jesus smiled at them.

"Peace be with you," he said, and gently he told them to come to him and touch him to make sure he was real. The disciples were so happy, they just didn't dare believe he was alive, even when they touched him! Jesus knew they needed a bit more proof that he was real.

"Have you got anything to eat here?" Jesus asked them. The disciples had been having a meal just before Jesus appeared. They looked at the table. There was some fish left. Jesus had often eaten fish with them. One of the disciples brought a piece of cooked fish from the table and gave it to Jesus. Jesus took the fish and ate it so they could all see. Now the disciples were really happy. Ghosts don't eat fish! Jesus was really alive – what a wonderful surprise!

The Resurrection

Questions to ask about the story:

- Why do you think the disciples thought Jesus was a ghost? [*Had seen him die, at least one of them had, and the doors were locked and hadn't opened to let him in.*]

- What did Jesus do to help them understand he was real and alive? [*Let them touch him and he ate something in front of them.*]

- Why do you think Jesus wanted his friends to know he was real? [*Proof of resurrection, not just ghost or vision, so they could be witnesses, tell others later.*]

- How do you think the disciples felt when they understood that Jesus was really there with them and really alive? [*Mixture of emotions, remind children of their own mixed feelings/reactions when given an enormous surprise.*]

- What questions do you think they asked Jesus?

- What might Jesus have replied?

- Who do you think the disciples would have told about seeing Jesus? [*Friends, family, disciples who were not there. Not the authorities, they were still scared of being caught.*]

Activities

1. **Work Book** page 24 'Jesus eats with the Disciples'.

2. Role-play: Imagine you were one of Jesus' friends in that room. Next day you meet a friend who wasn't there. Tell him/her what you saw and what you thought and felt.

3. Circle time or group discussion. Imagine you were in the room when Jesus appeared. What would you have said to him? What questions would you have asked him?

4. A group could paint a picture or make a collage of the risen Jesus for display and the children's questions or greetings to him could be printed and displayed round him.

5. **ICT for children:** www.request.org.uk Select 'Infants' then 'Festivals' then 'Easter' then 'Tell me about ... Easter'; also PDF 'Easter Worksheet' for sequencing activity.

   http://www.ngfl-cymru.org.uk/vtc/ngfl/re/b-dag/ngfl-container/re-unit2-en.html

The Resurrection

Jesus and Thomas

> Know that Thomas did not believe Jesus was alive.
> Reflect on the times when we don't understand what is happening.

Scripture text and notes for Teachers

Jesus appears to Thomas
Thomas, called the Twin, who was one of the Twelve, was not with them when Jesus came. When the disciples said, 'We have seen the Lord', he answered, 'Unless I see the holes that the nails made in his hands and can put my finger into the holes they made, and unless I can put my hand into his side, I refuse to believe'. Eight days later the disciples were in the house again and Thomas was with them. The doors were closed, but Jesus came in and stood among them. 'Peace be with you' he said. Then he spoke to Thomas, 'Put your finger here; look, here are my hands. Give me your hand; put it into my side. Doubt no longer but believe.' Thomas replied, 'My Lord and my God!' Jesus said to him:
'You believe because you can see me. Happy are those who have not seen and yet believe.'
(Jn. 20: 24-29)

Notes: The aim here is to keep the dual focus on how we always prefer to have first hand proof for believing things, but that we have to take a lot of things as true on other people's evidence.

KEY QUESTIONS (To share with children at any point)
Why do you think Thomas didn't believe that Jesus was alive?
What do you think made him change his mind?

Introductory Activity

Teacher helps children to understand that there are some things we believe that we cannot see or understand.

Invite children to think of things that we can see that are true and then, some things that are true that we cannot see.

Play the game I CAN SEE/CANNOT SEE for example:
There is a boy called ….. in the classroom.
How do you know?
The tree outside has roots.
How do you know? Because it would not grow without them, etc.
Other people have told us because they have seen roots.

The Resurrection

Link Sentence
Now we are going to hear about someone who heard some good news but did not believe it.

Text to read to children:
David and Jenny were arguing.

"It's true!" said Jenny. She felt a bit cross that her brother wouldn't believe her. "It's true! Uncle Jim is here and he's going to take us to the seaside today!"

David still wouldn't believe her.

"Uncle Jim lives in America," he said. "He can't be here."

Granny came and spoke gently to David.

"It's true," she said. "Come and see." And she took the children into the house with her. Guess who was waiting inside for them!

After a very happy day with Uncle Jim, the children were tired. Granny took them up to bed.

"I'm sorry I didn't believe you," David said to Jenny, "It just seemed too good to be true!"

"Don't worry," said Granny. "Even Jesus' friends found it hard to believe good news sometimes."

And as the children snuggled down in bed, she told them about Jesus' friend Thomas.

Questions to ask about story:

- Why didn't David believe Jenny? [*Thought she was making it up, seemed too good to be true, seemed unlikely, hadn't seen for himself*].

- Was there a time when you found something hard to believe? [*Children may refer back to the incredible facts of the introductory activity, or to their own experiences*].

- What made you believe it? [*Trust in person telling them, saw for themselves, other people assured them it was true*].

The Resurrection

Look again at picture on page 26 in Big Book and focus on Thomas: Jesus appears to the disciples.

Jesus with Thomas

Explain: Thomas was not present when Jesus appeared to the other disciples. He did not believe what they told him? Sometimes it is hard to understand what is going on. It was like this for Thomas, so Jesus helped him to understand. When we don't understand we can ask Jesus to help us.

More questions to ask about the picture on page 26 in the Big Book

- What do you think Jesus is saying to Thomas?

- What do you think Thomas is saying to Jesus?

- What do you notice about Jesus' hands?

Link Sentence
Today, we are going to hear how one of Jesus' friends did not believe he was alive, and how Jesus helped him to understand.

Text to read to children
Do you remember when Jesus appeared to his friends, the disciples, in the Upper Room? Well, one of the disciples wasn't there that day. His name was Thomas. When he came back, all the others were very excited. They couldn't wait to tell Thomas that Jesus was alive and they had seen him. Thomas didn't believe a word of it. "That's too good to be true!" he said. "I don't believe you."

"It's true," all his friends told him, but Thomas wouldn't change his mind.

"I would have to see Jesus with my own eyes, and touch him with my own hands," he said. "I can't believe he's alive unless I do that."

The next week the disciples were all together again in the same room, and this time Thomas was with them.

Suddenly, Jesus was in the room again with them.

"Peace be with you," he said. And then he looked at Thomas.

The Resurrection

"Come here, Thomas," he said, gently. "Look at me and touch my hands."

Thomas knew it was really Jesus, really alive.

"My Lord and my God," he said, and all the disciples knew he believed them now.

Jesus looked at Thomas again.

"You believe I am alive because you have seen me and touched me," he said. "There will be lots of people who are blessed because they believe I am alive without being able to see me and touch me."

Questions to ask about picture and story:
- Why do you think Thomas didn't believe his friends when they told him they had seen Jesus? [*Too good to be true, people don't come back from the dead.*]

- What made Thomas believe Jesus was really alive? [*He saw and heard and touched Jesus.*]

- Why do you think Jesus thought it was important that Thomas and the other disciples believed he was alive? [*So they could tell other people they had really seen and touched Jesus, so they could believe.*]

- Who do you think Jesus was talking about when he said there would be lots of people who believe he is alive even though they didn't see him or touch him? [*Us!*]

Activities
1. **Work Book** page 25 'A big surprise for Thomas'

2. a) Invite children to share what we believe about the Resurrection of Jesus. Write statements on white board.

   b) Use additional statements in **Teacher's Book** on page 110 to help. Cut out the statements and put them on strips of coloured cards together with the children's statements.

   c) Use image of a cross in **Teacher's Book** on page 111 to photocopy to size A3 for prayer service or use a crucifix. Invite the children to Blu Tack all statements to the paper cross or around a crucifix.

   d) Children stand around the cross and sing 'I am here with you' track 6 Disc 2 on CD 'More Stories and Songs of Jesus' or another Resurrection song.

ICT for children: www.reonline.co.uk Click on 'God' to hear story of birth, life, death & resurrection of Jesus.

The Resurrection

Jesus returns to Heaven

> Know that Jesus returned to heaven after forty days.
> Reflect on the promises he made to us.

Scripture text and notes for Teachers

Last instruction to the apostles
"Then Jesus told them, 'This is what I meant when I said, while I was still with you, that everything written about me in the Law of Moses, in the Prophets and in the Psalms, has to be fulfilled'. He then opened their minds to understand the scriptures, and he said to them, 'So you see how it is written that the Christ would suffer and on the third day rise from the dead, and that, in his name, repentance for the forgiveness of sins would be preached to all the nations, beginning from Jerusalem. You are witnesses to this'.

'And now I am sending down to you what the Father has promised. Stay in the city then, until you are clothed with the power from on high.'" (Lk. 24:36-43)

The ascension
"Now, having met together the apostles asked Jesus, 'Lord has the time come? Are you going to restore the kingdom of Israel?' He replied, 'It is not for you to know the times or dates that the Father has decided by his own authority, but you will receive power when the Holy Spirit comes on you, and then you will be my witnesses not only in Jerusalem but throughout Judea and Samaria, and indeed to the end of the earth'.

As he said this he was lifted up while they looked on, and a cloud took him from their sight." (Acts 1:6-9)

Notes: Jesus will send his Spirit to all who believe in him (Jn. 14:16-17). Jesus will come back and take us with him to heaven (Jn. 14:3).

Change of name: It was about this time that the name disciple changed to 'apostle'.

KEY QUESTIONS (To share with children at any point)
Why do you think Jesus had to go back to heaven?
What do you think God said to Jesus when he went back to heaven?
What do you think his friends thought when he left?

Introductory Activity
Talk about people leaving and promising to return - perhaps leaving something as a

The Resurrection

kind of pledge - you look after this till I come back. Objects could be shown - Auntie so-and-so left this for me to look after because I was sad when she left - but I know she will come back - she promised - I am looking after this till she comes back. Or it could be a short story along those lines.

Link Sentence
Today, we are going to hear how Jesus returned to God his Father in heaven, and how his friends were there to say goodbye.

Look at the picture on page 26 in Big Book: The Ascension

One day, Jesus took his disciples up on a hill.

Jesus told them that he had to go back to God.

He reminded them of things he had taught them.

He promised to send the Holy Spirit to help them.

Questions on Big Picture
Who do you see?
Where are they?
What are they doing? Why?
What do you think has happened? How do you know?

Text to read to children
It was forty days since that first Easter Sunday when Jesus rose from the dead. His friends were very happy. Lots more people saw Jesus alive again and everyone was amazed.
But the time went by very quickly. On the fortieth day, Jesus said to his friends, "Come with me." He led them out of the big city of Jerusalem to a quiet place. He explained to them that he had to go back to God his Father in heaven, and he reminded them of the things he had taught them. Then Jesus gave them some promises and some instructions, and a blessing.

The Resurrection

This is what Jesus promised his friends:
- You are going to be witnesses so everyone will know I rose from the dead.
- The Holy Spirit will come to you.
- He will give you power so you're not afraid to tell people about me.
- He will help you remember all I said.
- He will help you to think of the right words to say.

This is what he told his friends to do:
- Go back to Jerusalem.
- Stay in the city until the Holy Spirit comes.

As Jesus finished speaking it became very cloudy in the place where they were, and gradually the disciples could not see Jesus at all. They were still trying to see into the cloud when they noticed that two men dressed in white were standing there.

"Why are you standing there looking up to heaven?" the men said. "Jesus has gone back to heaven, but one day people will see him return."

The disciples went straight back to Jerusalem and stayed there as Jesus had asked them. They waited and prayed: they had a lot to think about.

Questions to ask about the story:

- What do you think the disciples thought when they realised Jesus was going back to heaven?
  [Couldn't believe they were going to lose him a second time, wondered how he would get there, wondered if he would die again, lonely, cross.]

- Can you remember the promises Jesus made to his disciples when he went back to heaven?

- What did the disciples have to do when Jesus had gone?

- How do you think they felt? Why?

Activities
1. Make a tableau of the disciples looking up to the sky as Jesus left them.
   Ask the children: How do you think the disciples were feeling?
   What do you think will happen next?

2. **Work Book** page 26 'Jesus goes back to heaven'.

3. Prayers to Jesus: encourage the children to write their own.
   For example: Jesus, be with us; Jesus, help us; Jesus, we love you.

WE BELIEVE

Jesus died for us.

Jesus rose from the dead.

Jesus is alive.

Jesus is with us always.

We will be with Jesus in heaven.

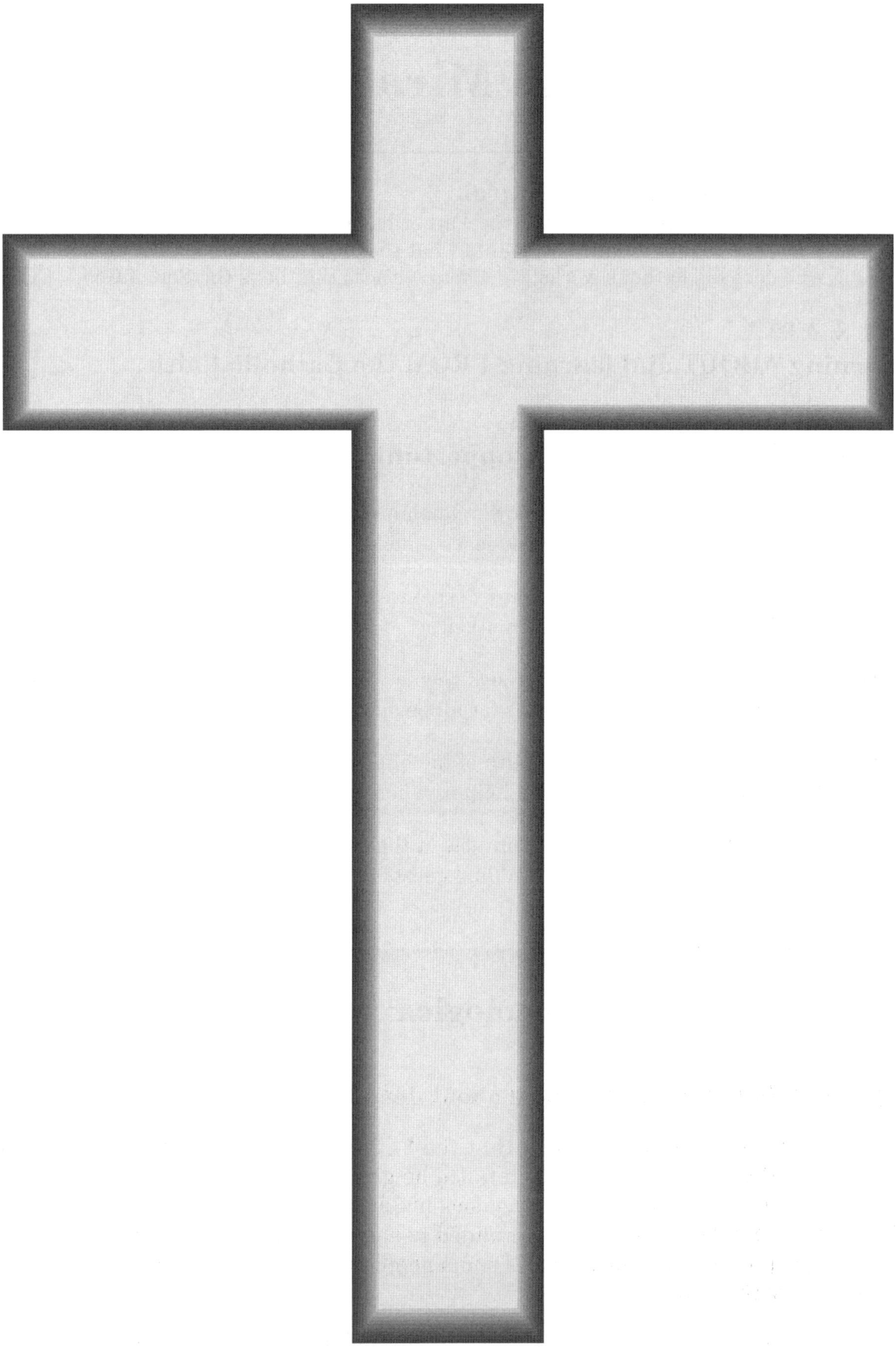

1.6 Miracles

Catechism of the Catholic Church
"The signs worked by Jesus attest that the Father has sent him. They invite belief in him. To those who turn to him in faith, he grants what they ask. So miracles strengthen faith in the One who does his Father's works; they bear witness that he is the Son of God." CCC 548

AT1 & AT2
Learning ABOUT and learning FROM the Catholic Faith

Key Learning Objectives
In this unit you will have the opportunity to:

- Know that Jesus showed his great power when he calmed the wind and the waves.
  - Reflect on the fact that we can ask Jesus to help us when we are afraid;

- Know that compassion motivates many people to act for the good of others.
  - Think about how we can help each other.

- Know that Jesus showed his love for sick people when he cured a man who was paralysed.
  - Reflect on the great love Jesus has for all people who are sick.

- Know that Jesus responded to the faith of the blind man with compassion.
  - Reflect on the fact that Jesus will help us when we pray to him.

- Hear how Jesus performed his first miracle at the request of his Mother.
  - Think about Jesus helping the wedding guests at Cana.

Theological Notes

Q. What do the miracles tell us about Jesus?

"The signs worked by Jesus attest that the Father has sent him. They invite belief in him. To those who turn to him in faith, he grants what they ask. So miracles strengthen our faith in the One who does his Father's works; they bear witness that he is the Son of God and are not intended to satisfy people's curiosity or desire for magic. Despite his evident miracles some people rejected Jesus; he is even accused of acting by the power of demons.

By freeing some individuals from the earthly evils of hunger, injustice, illness and death, Jesus performed messianic signs. Nevertheless he did not come to abolish all

Miracles

evils here below, but to free men from the gravest slavery, sin, which thwarts them in their vocation as God's sons and causes all forms of human bondage." CCC 548-549

Q. What should be stressed when teaching miracles to young children?
Miracles are signs – **signs of God's power**, worked because of God's compassionate and healing love; these **signs** call for and demand **'faith'**, though not always from the person who receives the miracle. (e.g Lazarus, Jairus' daughter.) They are seen as signs pointing to who Jesus is. Jesus has this power because he is God the Son. He showed his power because he wanted people to believe and trust in him.

Q. What is the importance of the miracle at Wedding at Cana in Galilee
"On the threshold of his public life Jesus performs his first sign - at his mother's request - during a wedding feast. The Church attaches great importance to Jesus' presence at the wedding at Cana. She, that is the Church, sees in it the confirmation of the goodness of marriage and the proclamation that thenceforth marriage will be an efficacious sign of Christ's presence." CCC 1613

The Storm at Sea

> Know that Jesus showed his great power when he calmed the wind and the waves.
> Reflect on the fact that we can ask Jesus to help us when we are afraid.

Scripture text and notes for Teachers

The calming of the storm
"Then Jesus got into the boat followed by his disciples. Without warning a storm broke over the lake, so violent that the waves were breaking right over the boat. But he was asleep. So they went to him and woke him saying, 'Save us, Lord, we are going down!' And he said to them, 'Why are you so frightened, you men of little faith?' And with that he stood up and rebuked the winds and the sea; and all was calm again. The men were astounded and said, 'Whatever kind of man is this? Even the winds and the sea obey him.'" (Mt. 8:23-27)

Notes: With very young children it is important to concentrate on the motive for miracles (usually compassionate love) rather than over-emphasising the supernatural element.

Miracles are not magic. Magic is about control, about illusion, a trick, whereas miracles are about power and faith.

KEY QUESTIONS (To share with children at any point)
Why do you think Jesus used his power to calm the storm?
Where do you think he gets this power?

Miracles

Introductory Activity
Circle time: Think of something you can do.
I can ....
Think of something you can do that a baby can't do.
Think of something a grown up can do that you can't do.

Link Sentence
Today, we are going to hear about what Jesus can do.

Look at picture on page 28 of Big Book: Miracles

> There is a bad storm on the lake.
>
> Jesus' friends are afraid.
>
> They wake Jesus to tell him.

Questions to ask on picture in Big Book
- What can you see in the picture?
- Have any of you ever been on a boat when the sea was stormy?
- How did you feel?

Text to read to children:
Jesus had been busy all day, teaching people beside the lake. It was a very big lake, so big it looked like the sea. Sometimes people called it the Sea of Galilee. When the evening came, Jesus turned to his friends who had a fishing boat. He asked them to take him to the other side of the lake.

The boat set off, but Jesus was very tired. He lay down on the big cushion at the back of the boat and fell fast asleep. The disciples sailed on, across the big lake.

Suddenly, a huge wind began to blow. It roared around the boat and made enormous waves on the water. The waves splashed so high that the boat began to fill up with water. Jesus' friends tried hard to keep the boat going, but it was no use. The boat was going to sink in the storm!

The disciples knew they must wake Jesus. He would help them.

"Wake up!" they shouted. "Save us, Lord, we sinking!"

Miracles

Jesus woke up. He spoke to the wind and to the waves.

"Peace!" he said. "Be still."

At once, the wind stopped blowing and the waves stopped splashing and everything was calm, quiet and still.

"Why were you afraid?" Jesus asked his friends. "Didn't you trust me?"

Jesus' friends were amazed to see Jesus had so much power that he could even make the wind and the waves do what he said. They wondered who Jesus really was.

Questions to ask about the story:

- What did you think when you heard this story?

- How did the disciples feel when the storm came? What did they do? *[Frightened, tried to keep the boat afloat, tried to manage without Jesus.]*

- How would you have felt?

- Why do you think they woke Jesus? *[Fear, thought the boat would sink and they would drown; knew he was powerful.]*

- Why did he stop the storm? *[To help his friends, to show them who he was, to help them trust him.]*
  Could you have done that?
  Could the head teacher do it?
  Could Father. .... do it?
  Could a king or queen do it?

- What made Jesus so powerful that he could tell the wind and waves to stop, and they did? *[He was the Son of God, he made the wind and the waves!]*

- What do you think might have happened if the disciples had not woken Jesus? *[Lots of possibilities – children can simply say what they think. We can never know, of course.]*

Activities
1. Listen to the account of 'Jesus makes the wind stop blowing' CD 'More Stories and Songs of Jesus'.

2. **Work Book** page 27 'The Storm at Sea'.

Miracles

3. Children work in pairs: one is a disciple and the other interviews him/her.
   Prompt questions:
   - How did you feel when the storm started?
   - What did you do?
   - What did Jesus say?
   - How did you feel after Jesus had calmed the storm?
   - Where do you think Jesus gets this power from?

5. Use 'storm' music (Beethoven's Sixth Symphony) and let the children make a storm with instruments.

6. Sing and act the song **'Jesus, Help us'** CD 'More Stories and Songs of Jesus'.

7. We can trust Jesus any time when we are afraid. The children should understand that Jesus may not take away whatever is making them afraid but he will give them the strength to cope in the situation. Children can think of some situations when they could ask Jesus for help and that help may come in different ways. Think about ways in which Jesus' help might come, e.g. sometimes he works through other people.
   Imagine some situations where help might be needed:
   a. It is your first day at somewhere new [swimming club, a new school] and you do not know anyone. You would rather stay at home.
   b. Someone in another class keeps picking on you at playtime.
   c. There's a bad storm outside and the thunder is really loud.
      Suggest what kind of help Jesus might give you. *(Courage, a good idea, speak to someone etc.)*

ICT for children: www.request.org.uk Select 'Infants' then 'The Life of Jesus' then 'Tell me a story' then 'The Storm on the Lake'.

Helping Others

Begin to understand how compassion motivates many people to act for the good of others. Reflect on how we help one another.

Note for Teachers

Notes for Teacher
We all have mixed motives for helping, as with any human action. In this unit the focus is on compassionate action taken for the good of others in spite of feelings to the contrary or ulterior motives.

Miracles

KEY QUESTIONS (To share with children at any point)
How do you think we can help other people?
Why do you think people help each other?

Introductory Activity

Make a display of people helping each other. Help children to think of a time when they have helped someone in need. Encourage them to focus on times when someone else needed help, rather than those times when the child was being helpful simply by doing what s/he ought to have been doing. Children could either paint a picture of this for the display, or bring in an object which reminds them of this time, for example, a cup to show how they fetched someone a drink.

Link Sentence
Today, we are going to hear how some children helped each other and think about why they did that.

Look at page 29 in Big Book: Kris is hurt

> Kris has fallen and hurt his leg. He is not able to stand up.
>
> His friends want to help him. What can they do?

Question on picture in Big Book
- What do you think is happening in this picture?

Text to read to children:

Kris was feeling very grown up. His mum said he was old enough to go to the shop on the corner all by himself. He decided to go and buy some sweets.

Kris set off with his money in his pocket.

"Come straight back," called his mum.

At the shop there was a big queue, but Kris didn't mind. It meant he had lots of time

Miracles

to look round the shop. At last, he chose his sweets and paid for them. "I'd better hurry back home," he thought, and ran out of the shop and along the pavement as fast as he could. He didn't see the pile of slippery leaves and paper ahead of him.

Crash! Kris slipped over and fell down really hard. He couldn't get up, his leg hurt so much. Kris was trying not to cry and wondering what he should do when he heard footsteps. Two girls from his class at school hurried up to him.

"Your leg looks really bad," one of them said. "Shall I put a clean tissue over it?"

The other girl looked down the road.

"You live just down there don't you?" she said. "Shall I go and get your Mum?" And she ran off.

The first girl stayed with Kris until her friend got back with his mother.

"We hope you feel better soon," they said as they went on their way.

Questions to ask about story:

- Why did Kris need help? *[Hurt, couldn't help himself.]*

- Why do you think the two girls stopped to help him? *[They knew him and felt sorry for him or, they knew it was the right thing to do even if they didn't like him. They might have fallen over themselves and knew what it felt like, also may have enjoyed feeling important, getting attention, our motives are often mixed, but it is doing what we know is right that is important.]*

- Do you think everyone would have done what the girls did? Why/why not? *[Some might have ignored him, told someone, but not helped him nthemselves]*

- What help might Kris have needed which the girls couldn't give? *[Carrying him home, taking him to hospital, make the point that they did what was in their power to do.]*

Activities
1. Role-play some situations with alternative endings where a child could help someone in need. This could be done twice for each one, with recognition of the choice people have to help, or not. Discuss why the child chose to help, or chose not to.

2. Make a class book on 'Why we help each other'. Put a large title on the cover – this could be done on computer by one child. Fill the book with ideas, written,

Miracles

drawn or printed, of **why** a child can help someone in need. Make sure the ideas are realistic – something a child can really choose to do, like choosing to play with a new or unpopular child for one playtime a week.

3. Take photos of children helping each other (spontaneously if possible). Invite children to write what they were doing. Use photos and children's explanation for a display.

4. **Prayer service**: Jesus helps us to help others even if we don't always feel like it.

   Dear Jesus,
   We ask you to help us to be kind to others when we do not feel like it.
   We ask you to help us to think about those who are lonely.
   We ask you to help us to love everybody.
   We ask you to help us to think of ways to help at home and at school.

   Song: **God of Mercy**
   You are with us
   Fill our hearts with your kindness …
   CD Share the Light, Bernadette Farrell. Available from www.viewpoint24.co.uk
   FAX. 020 8692 0375

Cure of the Paralysed Man

Know that Jesus showed his love for sick people when he cured a man who was paralysed. Reflect on the great love Jesus has for all who are sick.

Scripture text and notes for Teachers

Cure of the man who was paralysed
"Now Jesus was teaching one day, and among the audience there were Pharisees and doctors of the Law who had come from every village in Galilee, from Judea and from Jerusalem. And the power of the Lord was behind his works of healing. Then some men appeared, carrying on a bed a paralysed man, whom they were trying to bring in and lay down in front of him. But as the crowd made it impossible to find a way of getting him in, they went up on to the flat roof and lowered him and his stretcher down through the tiles into the middle of the gathering, in front of Jesus. Seeing their faith he said, 'My friend, your sins are forgiven you'. The scribes and the Pharisees began to think this over. 'Who is this man talking blasphemy? Who can forgive sins but God alone?' But Jesus, aware of their thoughts, made this reply, 'What are these thoughts you have in your hearts? Which

Continued on next page…

Miracles

of these is easier to say: 'Your sins are forgiven you' or to say, 'Get up and walk'? But to prove to you that the Son of Man has authority on earth to forgive sins, he said to the paralysed man – 'I order you: get up, and pick up your stretcher and go home.' And immediately before their very eyes he got up, picked up what he had been lying on and went home praising God.

They were all astounded and praised God, and were filled with awe, saying, 'We have seen strange things today'." (Lk. 5:17-26)

Notes: Jesus saw the faith of those helping the paralysed man and heard their prayer. He not only healed the man, but restored his faith so that he could help other people through his own personal experience of having trusted in Jesus. In addition, Jesus forgave him his sins which showed that Jesus was not only true man but also God because only God can forgive sins.

Jesus had a special love for all those who were sick, either in mind or body. He healed many people who came to him or were brought to him. The Church continues his healing mission today, through prayer and care for the sick and above all in the Sacrament of the Sick.

Children are sometimes puzzled that all sick people are not cured, then or now. We need to emphasise that Jesus knows the best way to help each sick person – our role is to trust in God, pray for the sick and do what we can to help.

KEY QUESTIONS (To share with children at any point)
Why do you think Jesus cured sick people?
How do you think Jesus helps sick people now?

Introductory Activity

Ask children if they know someone who is unwell. *[This would need to be handled carefully if a child or close relative is seriously ill.]* Sometimes children find it hard to think of anyone – public figures could be mentioned, or people known to the staff.

Ask children to make a prayer card – the person's name, decorated, on one side, and a short prayer of the children's making on the other. Suggestions: 'Please help him', or 'Jesus comfort her'. Steer towards requests for blessing, help and comfort rather than explicit demands for good health.

Children can bring these prayer cards and place them in a suitable area – round a statue of Jesus would be ideal, or in front of a crucifix or picture of Jesus. Explain that this is one way of bringing sick people to Jesus today.

Link Sentence
Today, we are going to hear how Jesus helped someone whose friends asked for help.

Miracles

Look at picture on page 30 in Big Book:
Cure of the man who was paralysed

> The man lying down is very sick.
> He can't move by himself.
> His friends bring him to Jesus.

Questions on picture in Big Book
- What do you think is happening in the picture?

Text to read to children:

One day, Jesus was inside a house teaching people and telling them all about God. More and more people came to listen. Soon, there was no more room in the house, not even by the door. Everyone was squashed inside, listening to Jesus.

After a while, four men arrived. They were carrying their friend on a stretcher. He was very ill. He couldn't walk at all. But his friends had heard about Jesus. They knew he could help sick people and make them well again.

When they got to the house, they were very worried. There were so many people!

"There isn't room for even one of us," they said, "We won't be able to carry the stretcher inside at all."

Then one of the friends had a good idea.

"Let's go up on the roof!" he said. We can make a hole in the roof and lower him down – right in front of Jesus!"

Everyone thought this was a great idea. In that country, most of the roofs were flat and only made of dried mud. It would be easy to make a hole. So up the steps they went, very carefully. Soon they had made a big enough hole and very gently and carefully, they tied ropes on to the stretcher and let their friend down inside the house to Jesus.

When Jesus saw the man on the stretcher, he wanted to help him. He spoke gently and kindly to the man.

Miracles

"Get up," he said, "Pick up that stretcher and go home."
And the man did!
Everyone was amazed.
"We've never seen anything like that!" they said.

Questions to ask about story:

- Why do you think there were so many people in the house listening to Jesus? *[People loved him, wanted to listen to him]*

- Why did the friends of the sick man bring him to Jesus? *[Had heard Jesus could cure sick people, loved their friend and wanted to help him]*

- What do you think all the people listening to Jesus thought when they saw the sick man coming down through the roof? *[Cross because they were listening hard, angry because roof damaged, pleased because they thought they might see a miracle, surprised anyone would take so much trouble to see Jesus – variety of feelings]*

- Why do you think Jesus wanted to help the sick man? *[Because he was kind, loved people, wanted to help, because he wanted to show people he was God and had the power to heal, because he wanted to reward the faith of the friends who had brought the sick man]*

How can we help our friends who are sick? *[Doing practical things for them, visiting, writing letters, phoning, above all bringing them to Jesus in prayer and trusting him to help them in the best way for them.]*

Activities

1. Listen to the story '**Jesus heals a man who could not walk**' CD Stories & Songs of Jesus.

2. **Sing and act** out the story for assembly. Use song '**Walking Up to Jesus**' on CD Stories & Songs.

3. **Work Book** pages 28 (1) & 29 (2) 'The Man who could not walk'.

4. Ask children to create tableaux of how they can help their friends who are sick. These can be photographed and captioned, e.g. visit them, make a card, pray for them, etc.

5. **Prayer** to thank God for everyone who helps us:
   Dear God, We thank you for all the people who help us, mums, dads, teachers, etc.
   Dear God, we thank you for all the people who help those who are ill, doctors, nurses etc.
   Dear God, we thank you for all the people who feed the hungry.

Miracles

Cure of the Blind Man

> Know that Jesus responded to the faith of the blind man with compassion.
> Think of ways in which we can trust Jesus in situations of need.

Scripture text and notes for Teachers

The blind man of Jericho
"They reached Jericho; and as Jesus left Jericho with his disciples and a large crowd, Bartimaeus (that is, the son of Timaeus), a blind beggar, was sitting at the side of the road. When he heard that it was Jesus of Nazareth, he began to shout and to say, 'Son of David, Jesus, have pity on me'. And many of them scolded him and told him to keep quiet, but he only shouted all the louder, ' Son of David, Jesus, have pity on me'. And many of them scolded him and told him to keep quiet, but he only shouted all the louder, 'Son of David, have pity on me'. Jesus stopped and said, 'Call him here'. So they called the blind man. 'Courage,' they said, 'get up: he is calling you.' So, throwing off his cloak, he jumped up and went to Jesus. Then Jesus spoke, 'What do you want me to do for you?' 'Rabbuni,' the blind man said to him, 'Master, let me see again.' Jesus said to him, 'Go; your faith has saved you'. And immediately his sight returned and he followed him along the road."
(Mk. 10:46-52)

Notes: A true miracle takes place when God's power (sometimes through holy women and men of God) works something which cannot be explained by all the laws of science.

A miracle is never worked just for our curiosity or entertainment (like 'magic tricks') but to arouse and deepen faith in God and Jesus Christ. The focus here is on the blind man's trust in Jesus.

When we ask Jesus to help, we also need to have faith that he knows the best way to help us.

KEY QUESTIONS (To share with children at any point)
In what ways do you think Jesus helps us if we ask him?
How can we show Jesus that we trust him?

Introductory Activity
Asking for help: bring in an activity that children are unlikely to have tried which is hard, but not impossible, e.g. folding a paper hat or boat. Show children a finished product and, if possible, the process. When they have admired it, ask them what would happen if they were asked to do this. What would they need? *[They would need help as well as the materials.]*

Ask them about other activities where they need help, in any area. Discuss who helps them.

Miracles

Link Sentence
Today, we are going to hear how Jesus helped someone who trusted him.

Look at the picture on page 31 in Big Book: The Blind Man

> The man sitting by the road is blind.
>
> He calls to Jesus. He says, "Jesus, help me."
>
> What do you think will happen?

Question on picture in Big Book
- What do you notice about the man sitting on the ground?
- What is he saying?

Text to read to children:
Bartimaeus couldn't see. He was blind. That meant he couldn't work and that meant he couldn't buy food. Every day he sat huddled in his cloak by the side of the road leading into the town, begging the people who went past to give him something. Some of them did, and some of them didn't.

One day, he heard a great crowd of people coming along the road. Bartimaeus knew Jesus had been in town – he would be going past where Bartimaeus was sitting. Bartimaeus had heard that Jesus could cure sick people. Perhaps he would help him! It wouldn't do any harm to ask. Bartimaeus plucked up all his courage and began to shout as loudly as he could.

"Jesus, help me! Jesus, have mercy on me!"

He shouted so loudly, lots of people turned round and told him to be quiet, but he just shouted even louder. He just had to make Jesus hear him in that great crowd of people.

And Jesus did hear him, even though there were so many people talking to him on the road. He stopped.

"Call him here," Jesus said, and some people rushed over to Bartimaeus.

Miracles

"Cheer up," they said, "Come on, get up, he's calling you!"

At once, Bartimaeus got up, threw off his cloak, and went over to Jesus.

Jesus looked at him kindly.

"What do you want me to do for you?" he said.

"Master," said Bartimaeus, "I want to be able to see!"

Jesus knew that Bartimaeus trusted him. He trusted Jesus to decide whether he should see or not.

"Go on your way," Jesus said gently to him. "Your faith has made you well."

At once, Bartimaeus could see! And as the crowd following Jesus set off down the road again, I expect you can guess who was with them.

Questions to ask about the story:

- How do you think Bartimaeus felt as he sat at the side of the road every day? *[Sad, hungry, fed up, lonely.]*
- Why do you think he decided to ask Jesus for help? *[Heard he cured people, trusted him, willing to try anything]*
- What did Jesus ask him to do? *[Come to him]*
- What do you think Bartimaeus did when he could see again? *[Stayed with Jesus, told other people how Jesus healed him, perhaps was able to work again one day]*
- When Jesus uses his power to cure someone like this, we call it a miracle. Can you think of another miracle Jesus did? *[Calming storm, healing paralysed man, children may think of others.]*

Activities
1. **Listen** to story: 'Jesus heals a man who cannot see' CD Stories and Songs of Jesus.

2. **Act** and join in **song**: 'Bartimaeus' CD Stories and Songs of Jesus

3. **Work Book** page 30 'Bartimaeus'.

4. Jesus gives us people to help us. Talk about who they are: nurses, doctors, dinner ladies, etc.
   Children choose one or two to draw and write about.

ICT for children: www.reonline.co.uk Select 'Infants'; 'Bible'; New Testament then 'The Blind Man'.

Miracles

The Wedding at Cana

> Know that Jesus performed his first miracle at the request of his mother.
> Reflect on the fact that Mary our Mother, will ask Jesus to help us.

Scripture text for Teachers

The Wedding at Cana

"Three days later, there was a wedding at Cana in Galilee. The mother of Jesus was there, and Jesus and his disciples had also been invited. When they ran out of wine, since the wine provided for the wedding was all finished, the mother of Jesus said to him, 'They have no wine'. Jesus said, 'Woman, why turn to me? My hour has not come yet.' His mother said to the servants, 'Do whatever he tell you'.

There were six stone water jars standing there, meant for the ablutions that are customary among the Jews: each could hold twenty or thirty gallons. Jesus said to the servants, 'Fill the jars with water', and they filled them to the brim. 'Draw some out now,' he told them, 'and take it to the steward.' They did this; the steward tasted the water, and it had turned into wine. Having no idea where it came from – only the servants who had drawn the water knew – the steward called the bridegroom and said, 'People generally serve the best wine first, and keep the cheaper sort till the guests have had plenty to drink; but you have kept the best wine till now'.

This was the first of the signs given by Jesus: it was given at Cana in Galilee. He let his glory be seen, and his disciples believe in him." (Jn. 2:1-11)

KEY QUESTIONS (To share with children at any point)
What did Jesus do at the wedding?
Can you remember what his mother told the servants?
Did they do it?

Introductory Activity
List what you would like to have for your party.
Imagine there is not enough ... (cake, ice-cream etc.) how would you feel?

Link Sentence
Today, we are going to hear about a real wedding when the wine ran out and Jesus performed his first miracle.

Miracles

Look at the picture on page 32 in Big Book: The Wedding at Cana

> Jesus and his friends are at a wedding.
> Jesus' mother Mary is there too.
> But the wine has all gone and the party is not over!
> Mary tells Jesus about it.
> What will he do?

Questions on picture in Big Book:
- Who can you see in the picture?
- What do you think is happening?
- What do you think Mary is saying to Jesus?
- Can you imagine what Jesus will do? Why?

Text to read to children:

Have you ever been to a wedding? It's a very important occasion. The couple getting married and their parents want everything to be perfect for such an important day.

One day, Jesus and his mother Mary were invited to a wedding. Jesus' special friends, the disciples, were there too. The music was playing and everyone was enjoying themselves, drinking wine and dancing.

But there was a problem. There was not enough wine for everyone, and soon there was none left.

Mary noticed what had happened. She went to find Jesus.

"They have no wine," she told him. She knew Jesus would help.

Next Mary went to find the servants.

"Do whatever Jesus tells you," she said to them.

Jesus pointed to six great big water jars at the side of the room.

"Go and fill these with water," he said to the servants, "and then take some of the water in them to the man in charge of the feast.

So, the servants filled the jars with water and took some to the man in charge. He tasted it and he had a big surprise. The water wasn't water any more - it was

Miracles

really good wine! (I wonder if the servants were smiling - they knew what had happened!)

The man in charge sent for the bridegroom.

"You have saved the best wine till last!" he said.

Questions to ask about story:
- Have you ever been to a wedding or a party and something went wrong? How did people feel about that?
- How do you think the bride and bridegroom would have felt if they knew about the wine running out?
- How did Mary help when she saw the wine was all gone?
- What did Jesus tell the servants to do?
- Do you think they were surprised when they saw the water had changed into wine?
- Why do you think Jesus did this miracle? [*To help, to save embarrassment, to please his mother, to show his power, so people would know who he was.*]
- What do you think the wedding guests thought when they heard about the miracle?
- What do you think Mary wants us to learn from this miracle?

Activities
1. Children 'hot seat' one of the wedding guests: Ask them questions about what they saw. Then 'hot seat' Mary: What did she do? Why?

2. Retell the story of 'The Wedding at Cana'. *Extension:* Retell the story from another point of view, a guest, Mary, Jesus, the bridegroom.

3. Draw a scene from 'The Wedding at Cana' and then stick some speech bubbles above the picture and write in what the people might be saying

4. **Work Book** page 31 'Jesus goes to a Wedding'.

5. Listen to the story: 'Jesus goes to a Wedding', CD Stories & Songs of Jesus

6. Learn song: 'We will do what Jesus says', CD Stories & Songs of Jesus

7. Write a prayer to Mary, asking Jesus to help us. List the things that we would like Jesus to help us with.

8. **Work Book** page 32 'Jesus answers a prayer in different ways through people who help us'.
   Examples of the first picture could be doctors, nurses, etc.

Assessment for Learning

Good assessment should have variety, flexibility and be based on the professional judgement of the teachers. Most of the activities in the Teacher's Book and Pupil's Work Book could be used for assessment or schools may wish to develop their own.

Assessment should be integrated into teaching and learning. Tasks should allow children to demonstrate what they know, understand and can do. The key is to ask children good questions, allow time for them to think about their answers and probe for deeper meaning. Make sure children are challenged to think about situations and events so that they will learn to go beyond just repeating facts.

Assessment happens all the time. It can be formal or informal. The 'I can ...' statements on pages 130 to 131 are a guide to levels of achievement. They are only intended to be examples and can be easily adapted to suit content. The 'Key Questions' in each module can be used at any point and teachers will be able to gauge children's level of knowledge and understanding by their responses.

Not everything in religious education has to be assessed. The more personal aspect of some key learning objectives 'Learning FROM' AT2 cannot be assessed in the same way as 'Learning ABOUT' AT1.

The syllabus provides a clear statement of what is being taught and the less formal assessment is, at this stage, the more productive it is likely to be.

LEVELS OF ACHIEVEMENT

Attainment Target 1 (AT1) = Learning **ABOUT** the Catholic Faith

Attainment Target 2 (AT2) = Learning **FROM** the Catholic Faith

Range of levels within which the great majority of pupils are expected to work	Key Stage 1 Levels 1- 3
Expected attainment for the majority of pupils at the end of the key stage	Level 2

Guide to Levels of Achievement

KEY STAGE 1
ASSESSMENT FOR LEARNING

LEVEL 1

AT1
* I can tell the story of Noah and the Ark

* I can tell the story of the birth of Jesus.

* I can describe what happened when Jesus calmed the storm at sea.

* I can tell the story of the Good Samaritan.

* I can describe what happened to the man who could not walk.

AT2
* I can think of ways in which we can look after God's world.

* I can think of reasons why it is important to belong to God's family.

* I can make up a list of questions I would like to ask about the world.

* I can think of questions I would like to ask God about himself.

* I can tell you about my favourite person in the Christmas story.

Guide to Levels of Achievement

KEY STAGE 1
ASSESSMENT FOR LEARNING

LEVEL 2

AT1
* I can explain how you become part of God's family.

* I can explain why Mary and Joseph took Jesus to the Temple.

* I can tell the story of the Good Samaritan and explain the important message in it.

* I can give a reason why people go to church.

* I know what happened at the Resurrection and can give one reason why we celebrate Easter.

AT2
* I can think of reasons why we should look after God's world.

* I can think of some reasons why Jesus used his power to calm the storm at sea.

* I can describe how Jesus sometimes answers our prayers in different ways.

* I can suggest ways in which we can help other people.

Glossary for Pupil's

(This glossary will help children with the Work Book and the interactive activities on the website : www.tere.org)

Advent – The four weeks before Christmas when we get ready to celebrate Jesus' birthday.

Angel – A messenger from God.

Church
 a) All the people who love and believe in Jesus.
 b) The building where we go to praise God.

Flood – When lots of water covers the land.

Heal – To make someone better.

Heaven – Where God lives and where we hope to be with Him one day.

Hosanna – Save us, Lord!

Miracle – When God does something really wonderful that seems impossible.

Neighbour – Someone in our life who might help us or who might need our help.

Praise – When we tell someone how good we think they are.

Prepare – Get ready

Promise – When someone says they will be sure to do something.

Resurrection – When Jesus became alive again on Easter Sunday.

Temple – The special house God's people used to have for Him.

Trust – When we can be sure that someone will only do what is good for us.

World – The great big place where we all live.